CVC Storybooks

15 Reproducible Emergent Readers

Set 2

Stories and Pictures by Mark Linley

bartlebysbox.com

Dedicated to all teachers
and to the children in their care

ISBN 978-0-9977255-1-3

Contact:
    Mark Linley
    bartlebysbox@gmail.com

Dear Teacher,

Hello. My name is Mark Linley, the author and illustrator of the stories in this collection. I am a teacher with eighteen years of teaching experience in the primary grades. I use GUMDROPS for MOPPET TOPS books as a tool in my own classroom, as part of an extensive and well developed systematic early literacy program - a program which I have pieced together and developed myself over the course of my career.

These books have been part of my curriculum for many years and the kids love them. They love the stories, they love the pictures, they love the characters, and they love being able to page through a book and with varying degrees of effort, depending on the child, read every single word. These books work well for children just learning to read, who already know the alphabet and most of the sounds that the letters make. I have personally used these books with pre-kindergartners, kindergartners, beginning first graders, and as extended review for struggling first grade readers. They are easy and appropriate first steps for reading instruction. They will help you to get your students to read.

The GUMDROPS for MOPPET TOPS series was written and illustrated to fill a gap that I saw in the available literature. I created these books because I had students who needed to learn how to blend consonant-vowel-consonant (CVC) words and I was unable to find the right books to address that need. I developed the stories and drew the pictures myself; worked and reworked the drawings by hand and with digital editing software; wrote and rewrote the stories - changing an ending here, moving a page there, discarding stories altogether and writing new ones. These books have gone through many revisions over the years. May they serve you well.

With the GUMDROPS for MOPPET TOPS series, your students will be able read entire books without the frustrating experience of having to puzzle over whether to sound-out a word or to remember it iconically as a sight word. Children feel a sense of accomplishment after successfully reading a page and then moving on to the next page and reading that one too. They feel proud and confident when they are able to read a book by themselves all the way to the end. As a teacher it is a joy to witness the thrill felt by children who have books in their hands that they can read. Finally the kids have books that they can read all the way through!

Enjoy!

Sincerely,

Mark Linley

CONTENTS

PRINTING and ASSEMBLY

1. Copy and Print

For Copy Machines with a Double Sided Printing Option

[OPTION ONE]
Print booklets directly from your GUMDROPS for MOPPET TOPS Blackline Masters Compilation
1. Select two-sided printing on the menu of your copy machine.
2. Open your GUMDROPS for MOPPET TOPS Blackline Masters Compilation to the booklet you wish to print. Scan the page containing the *title page* and *back cover*.
3. Scan the next page in the Compilation, *booklet pages 1* and *10*.
4. Press print to test if both sides of the copy are oriented correctly. If not, re-scan both pages, ensuring that the second page is scanned the other way around.
5. Continue scanning until all pages of your booklet are copied.
6. Press print. All copies will have printed double sided.

[OPTION TWO]
Make MASTER COPIES of your booklets first
1. Copy and print each page of the booklet or booklets your wish to assemble.
2. Place your booklet or booklets in order into the document feeder of your copy machine, *with every other page oriented in the opposite direction*
3. Select the double sided printing option from your machine's menu.
4. Press print. All copies will have printed double sided.

For Copy Machines with a Single Sided Printing Option

A few preliminary *printing tests* will help to determine which way around you must refeed the printed paper for your particular printer or copy machine.

1. Copy and print the odd pages of the booklet you wish to assemble first; print the even pages separately. You will now have two stacks - a stack of odd pages and a stack of even pages.
2. Place the printed odd pages into your copy machine's paper feeder in the direction determined by your printing tests.
3. Place the stack of even pages into the document feeder.
4. Print. Your pages will now be printed double sided.

2. Stack

3. Cut

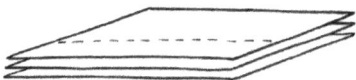

4. Fold and Staple

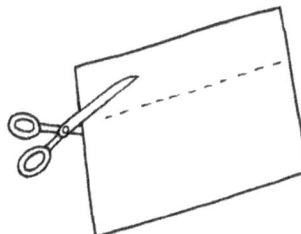

BOOKLETS

TAG

Story and Pictures by Mark Linley

SET 2.1

GUMDROPS for MOPPET TOPS

TAG

tag   cat
ran   cap

Got it!

bartlebysbox.com

cut

3

cut

1

tag

10

tag

bartlebysbox.com

ran

ran

cut

SET 2.1 - Book 1 - GUMDROPS FOR MOPPET TOPS

3

cut

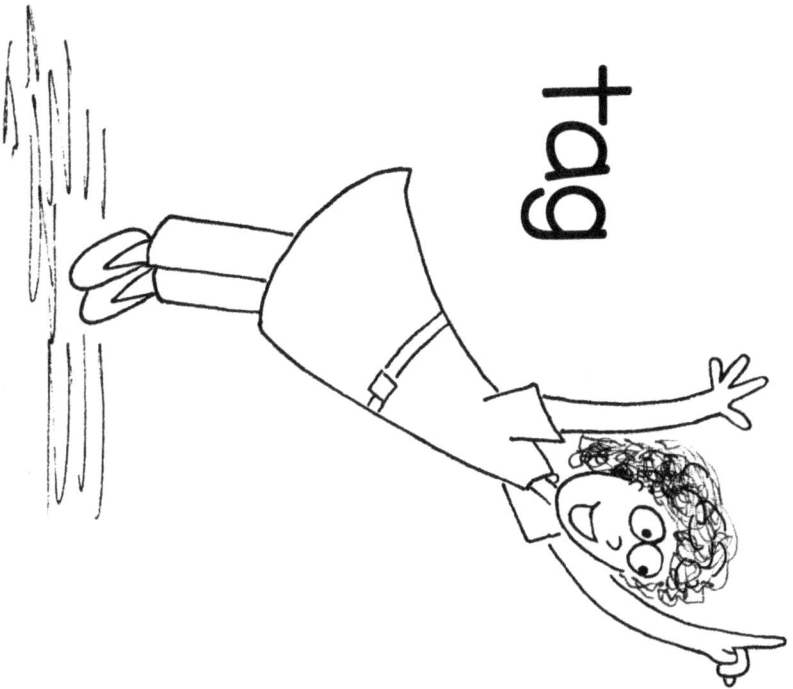

tag

8

cap

bartlebysbox.com

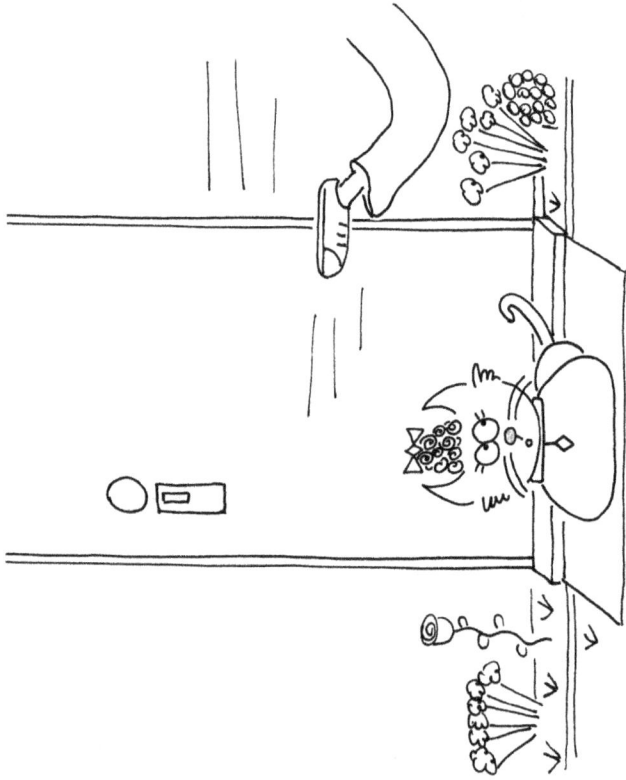

tag

4

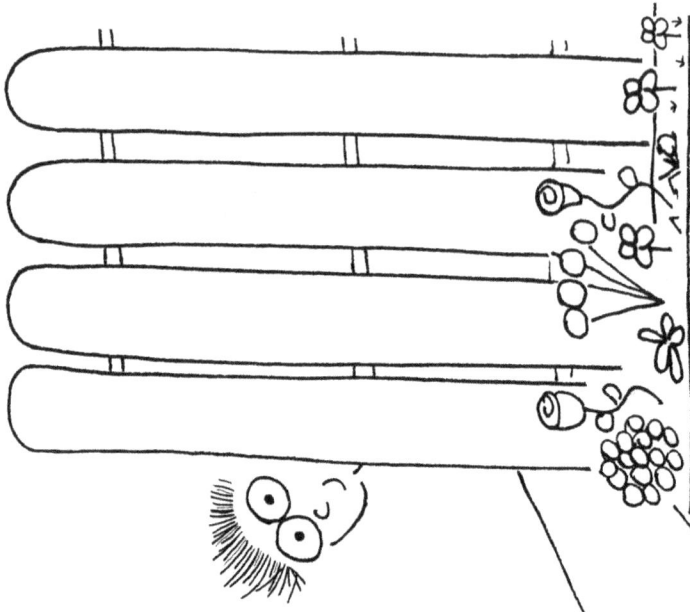

ran

7

cut

5

cut

ran

6

cat

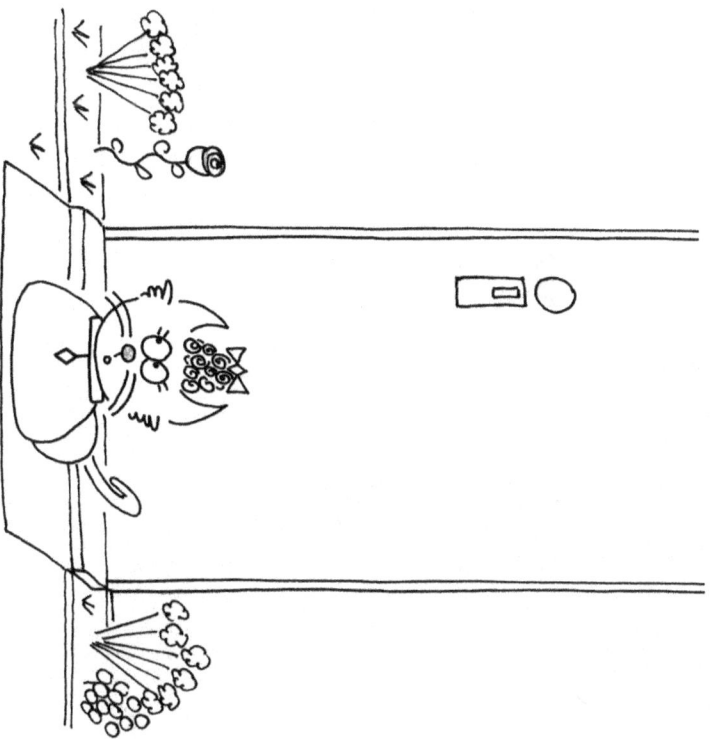

GET SET

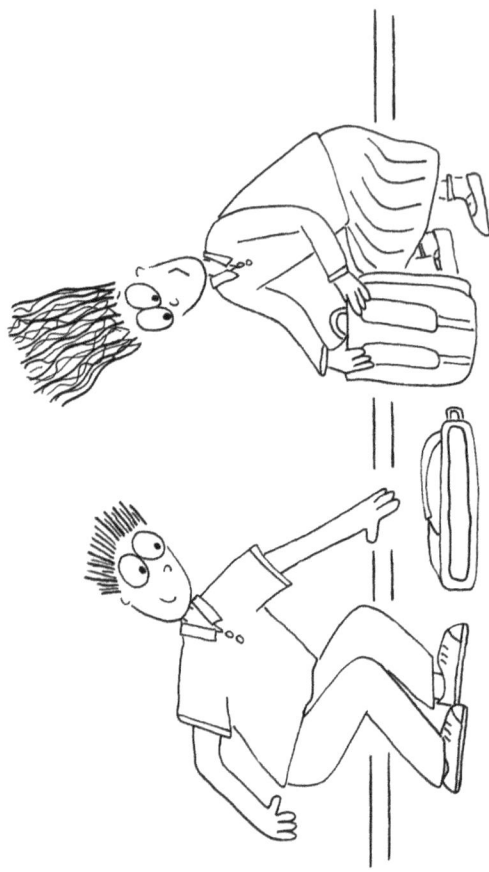

Story and Pictures by Mark Linley

SET 2.1

GET SET

bed   get
wet   fed
set   yes

Got it!

bartlebysbox.com

cut

9

I

cut

bed

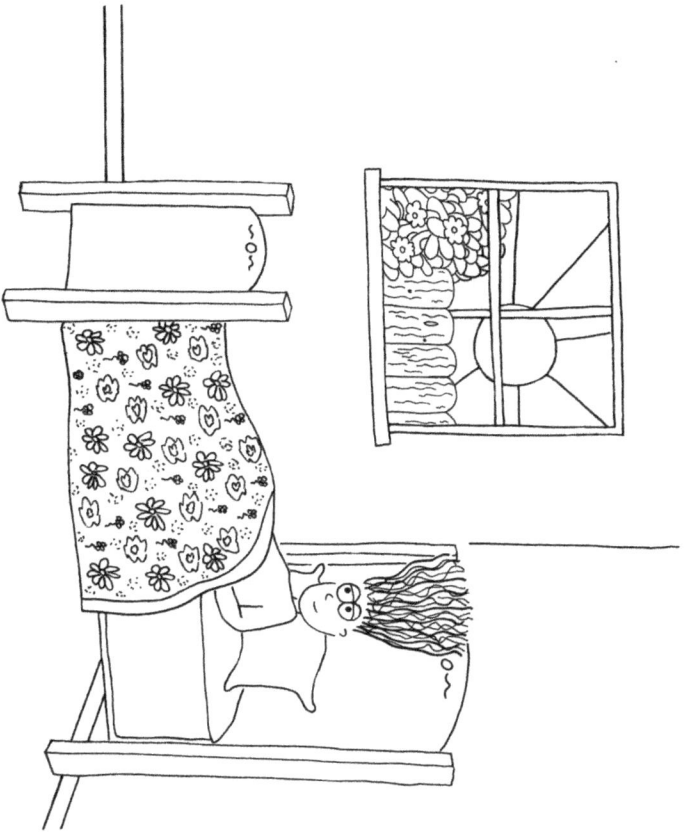

yes

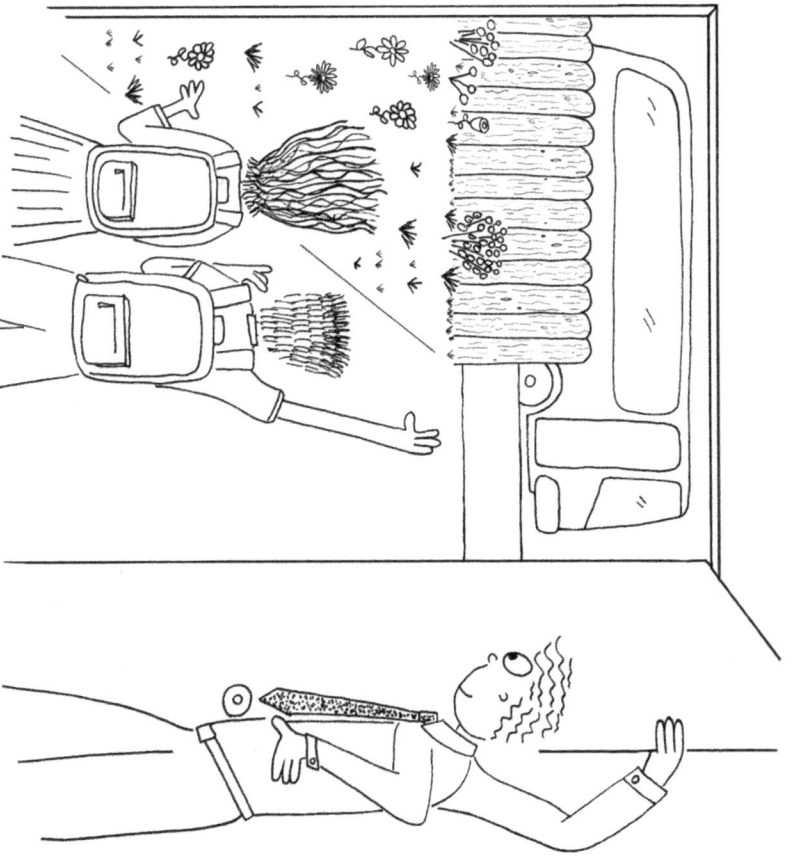

10

wet

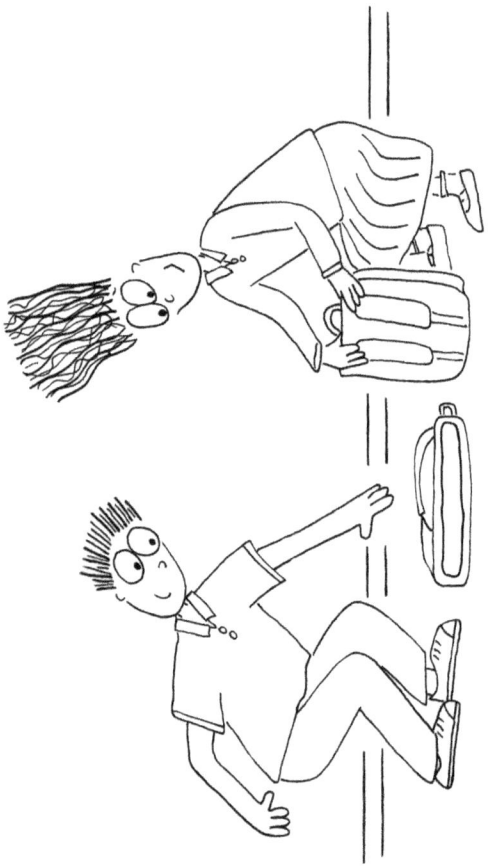

get

cut

3

cut

bed

3

8

yes

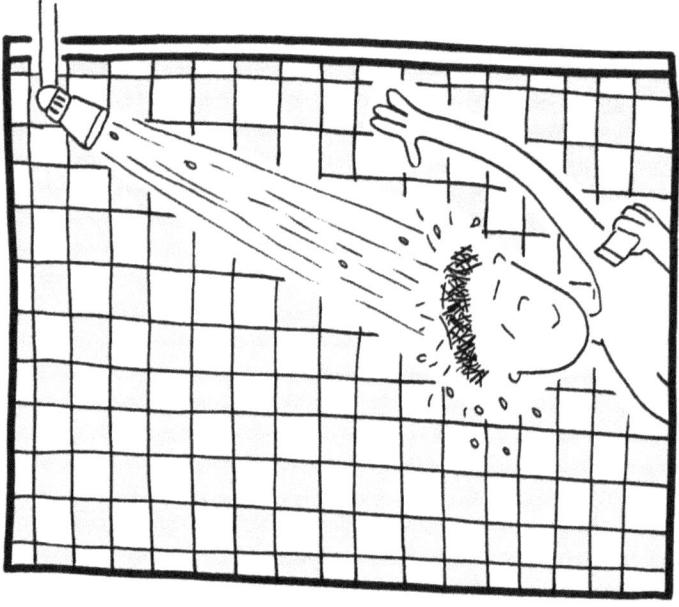

wet

4

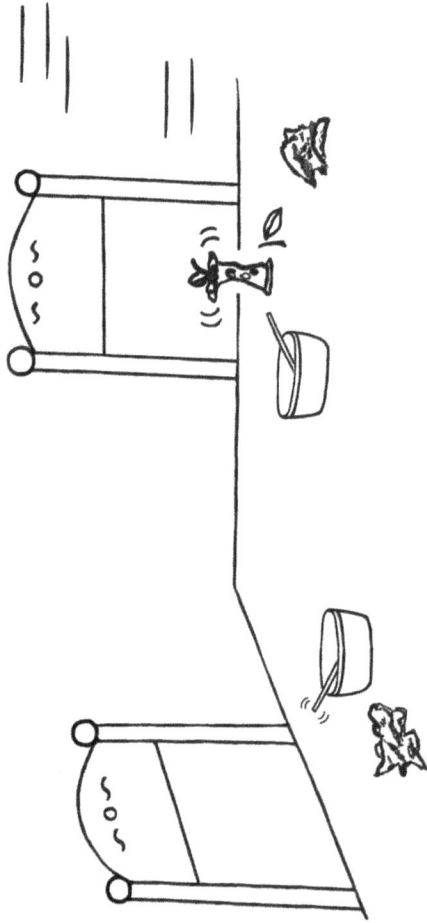

fed

7

cut

13

SET 2.1 – Book 2 – GUMDROPS FOR MOPPET TOPS

5

cut

set

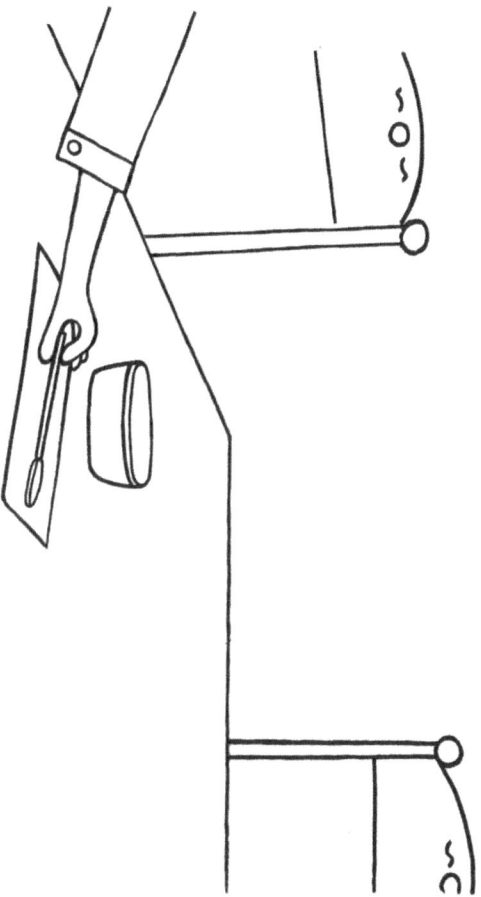

6

get

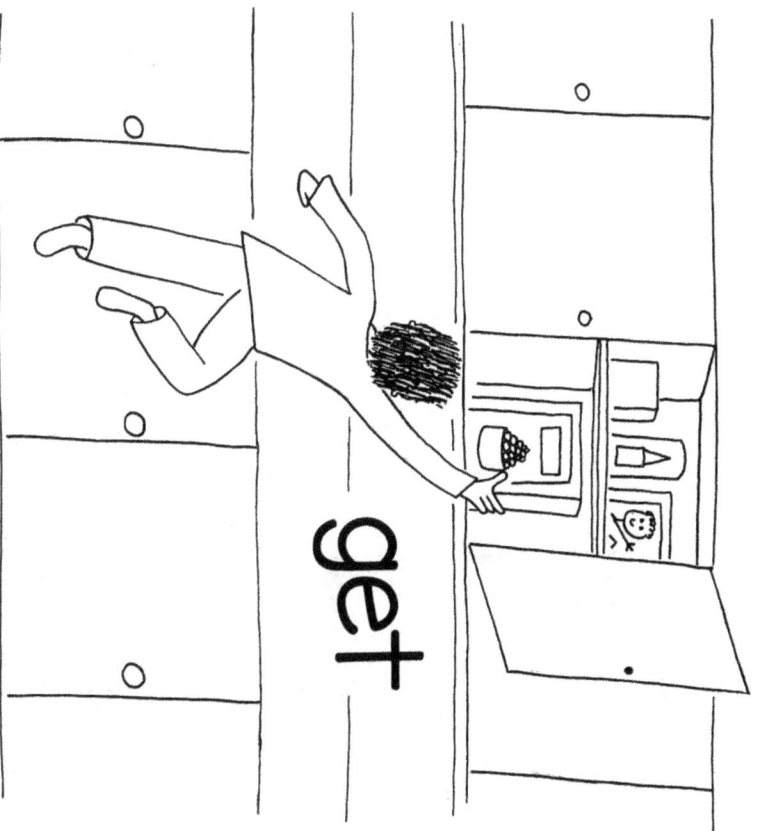

PIG IS IN

PIG IS IN

pig   in
sit   fin
sip   rip
zip   pin

Got it!

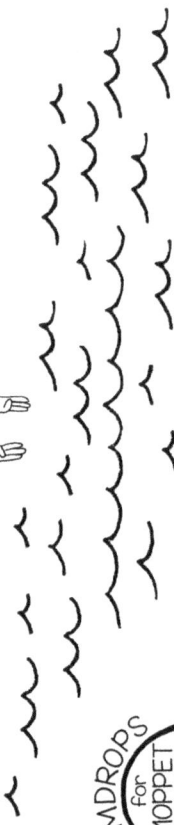

Story and Pictures by Mark Linley

GUMDROPS for MOPPET TOPS

SET 2.1

bartlebysbox.com

cut

cut

I

pig

pig

I0

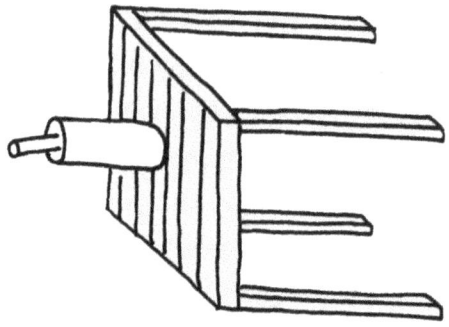

sit

2

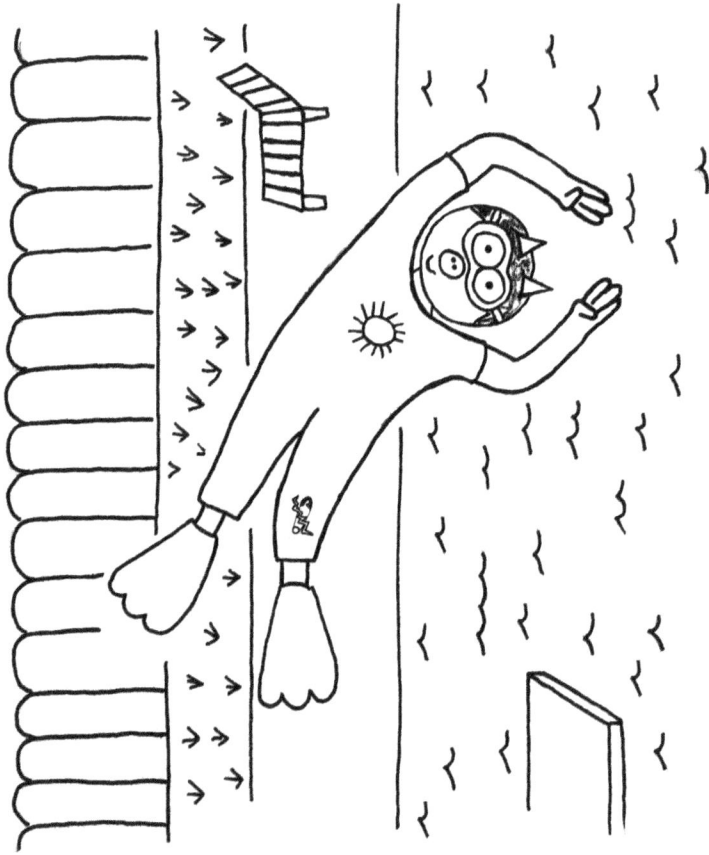

in

q

cut

SET 2.1 - Book 3 - GUMDROPS FOR MOPPET TOPS

3

cut

sip

3

pin

8

zip

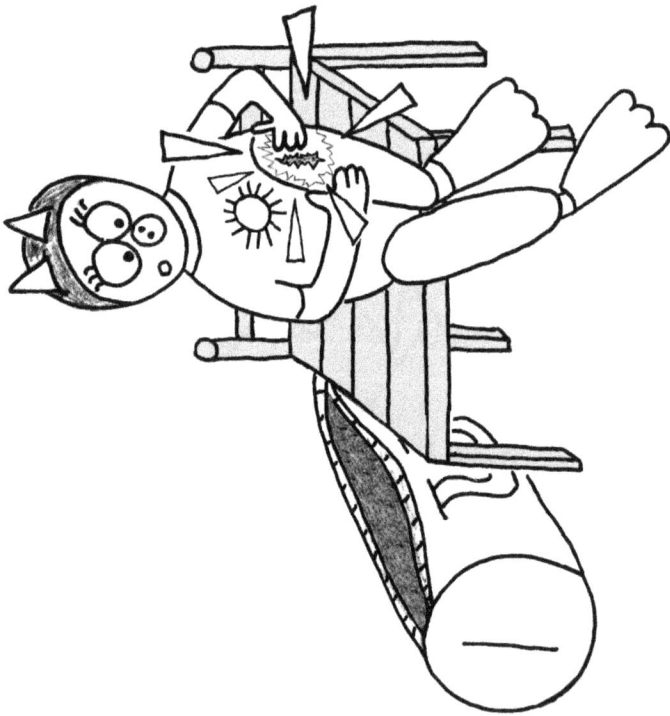

rip

cut

SET 2.1 - Book 3 - GUMDROPS FOR MOPPET TOPS

5

cut

in

fin

6

POP

Tom pot
Roz hot
Dot pop
Mom

Got it!

POP

Story and Pictures by Mark Linley

GUMDROPS for MOPPET TOPS

SET 2.1

bartlebysbox.com

cut

cut

I

Tom

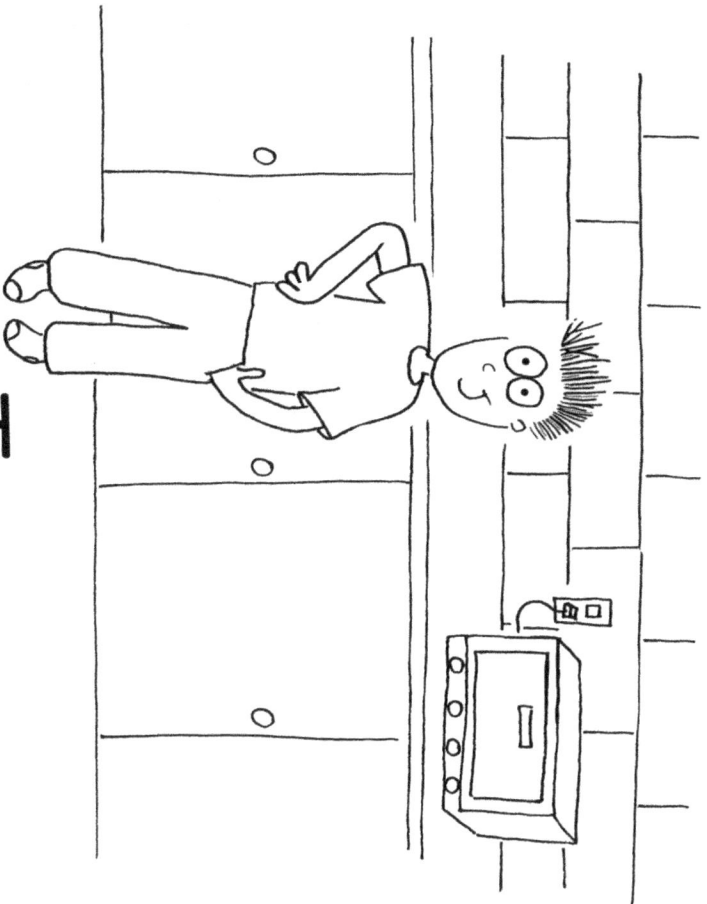

mmmm

IO

Roz

a 2

hot

b

cut

5

cut

pot

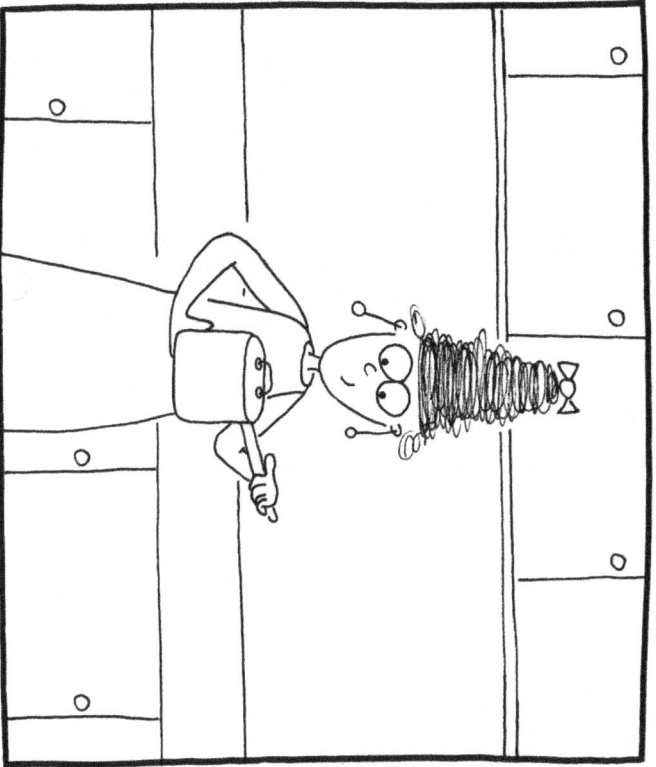

hot

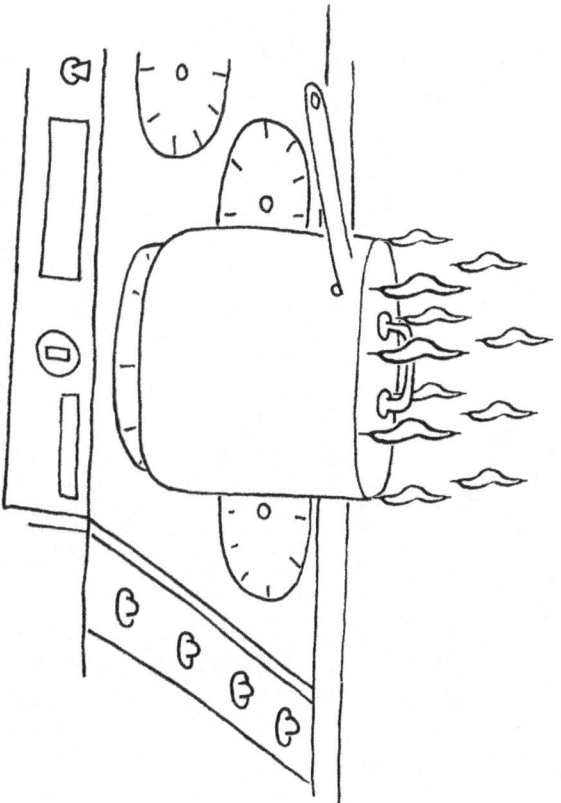

6

SUN FUN

Story and Pictures by Mark Linley

GUMDROPS for MOPPET TOPS SET 2.1

Copyright © 2017 by Mark Linley
All Rights Reserved
MADE IN THE USA

Got it!

SUN FUN

sun   run
up   fun

bartlebysbox.com

cut

27

cut

1

10

up

2

fun

q

cut

3

cut

run

8

up

up

4

run

7

cut

5

cut

fun

up

6

bartlebysbox.com

RAT CAN

Story and Pictures by Mark Linley

SET 2.2

RAT CAN

mat tap
pan rat
rag sat
nap

Got it!

bartlebysbox.com

cut

I

cut

mat

sat

10

bartlebysbox.com

pan

2

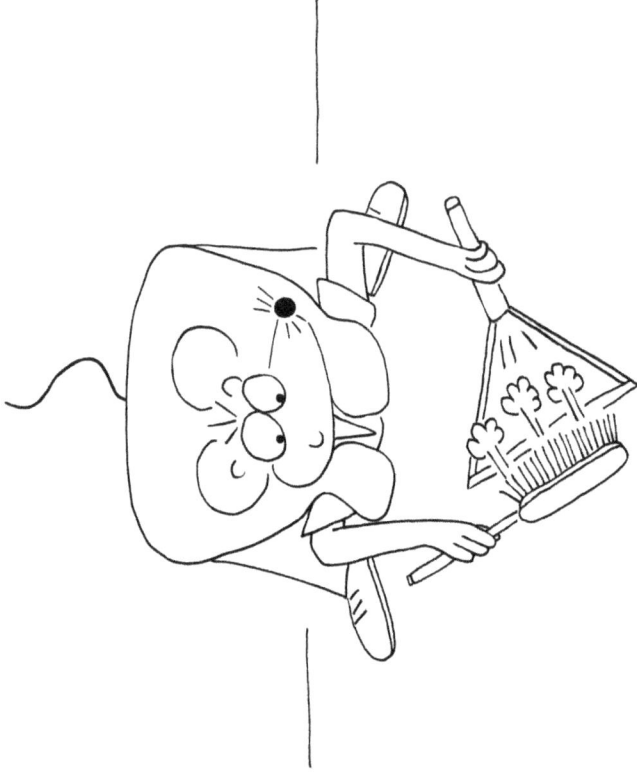

rag

q

cut

35

3

cut

rag

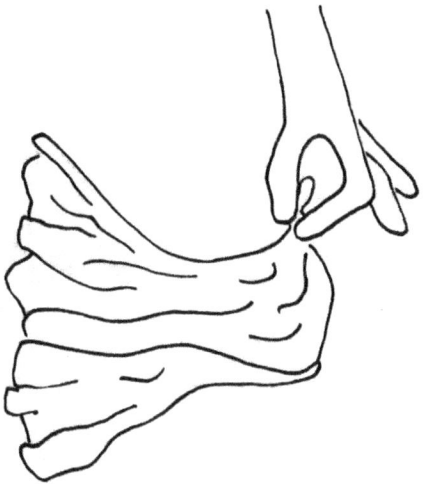

8

rag

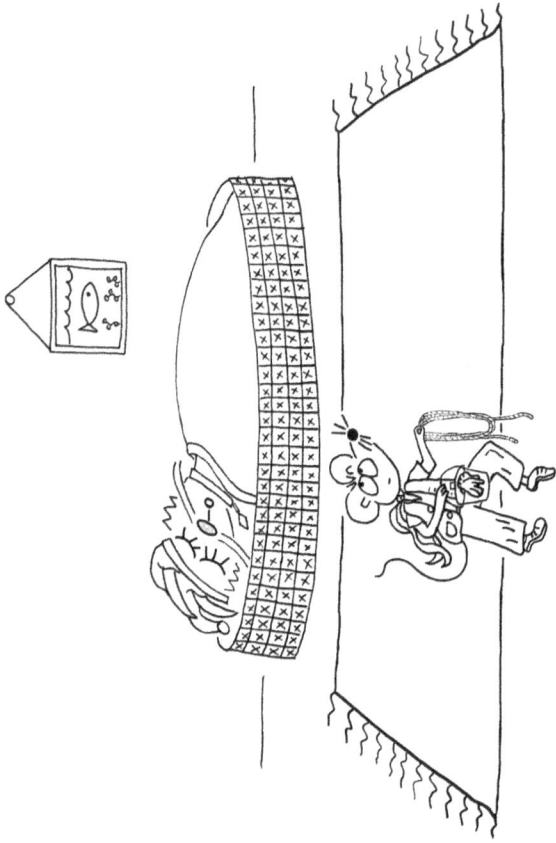

nap

4

rat

7

cut

SET 2.2 - Book 1 - GUMDROPS FOR MOPPET TOPS

5

cut

tap

6

rag

JET

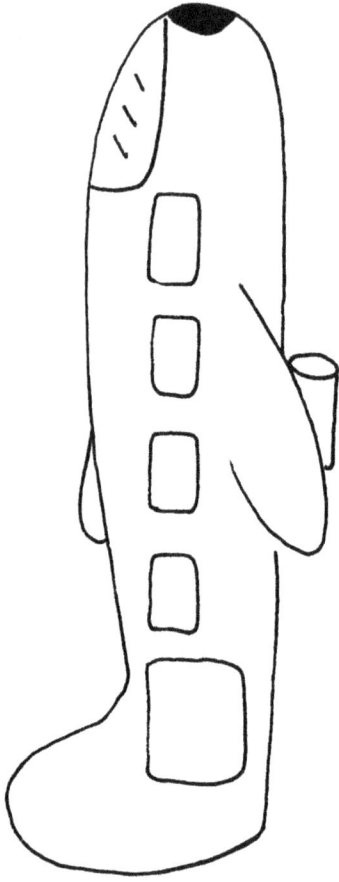

JET

bed men
jet net
leg yes

Got it!

Story and Pictures by Mark Linley

SET 2.2

GUMDROPS for MOPPET TOPS

bartlebysbox.com

cut

cut

I

bed

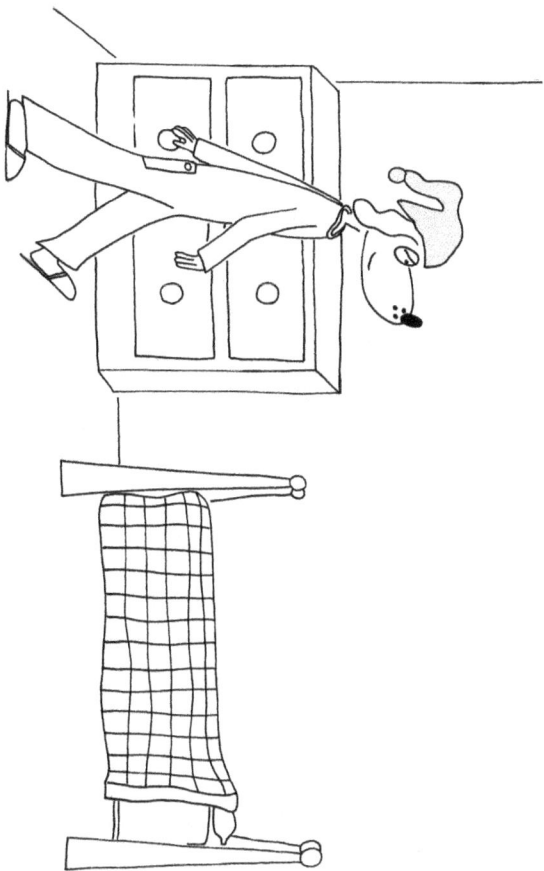

bed

10

ZZZZ

2

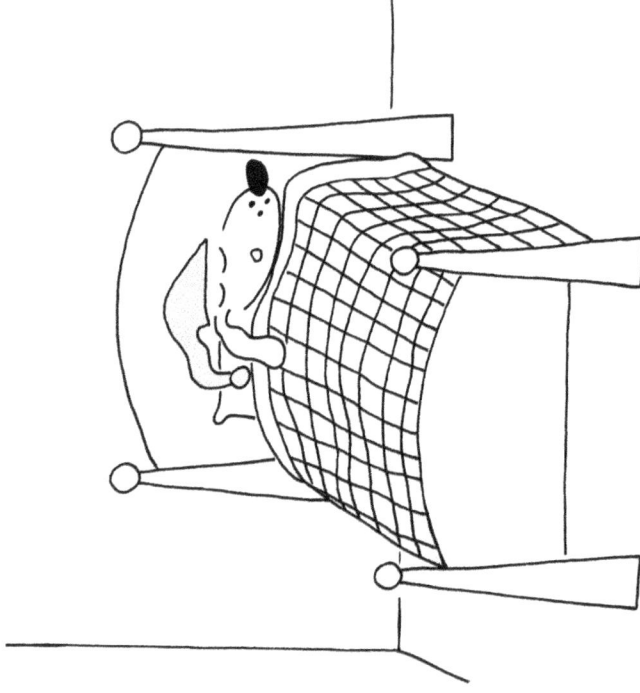

yes

q

cut

SET 2.2 - Book 2 - GUMDROPS FOR MOPPET TOPS

3

cut

jet

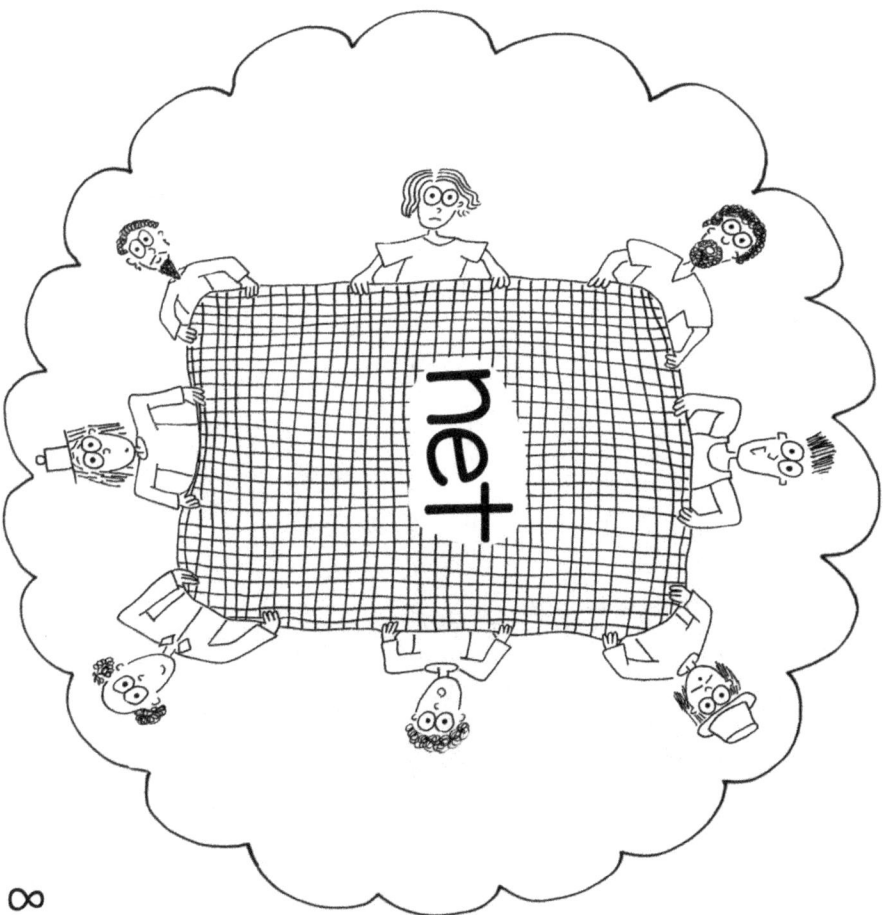

net

3

8

bartlebysbox.com

bed

4

men

7

cut

5

cut

leg

6

bed

KIDS

KIDS

fit
fix
in

lid
tip
sit
big

Got it!

Story and Pictures by Mark Linley

GUMDROPS for MOPPET TOPS

SET 2.2

bartlebysbox.com

cut

45

I

cut

lid

sit

I

10

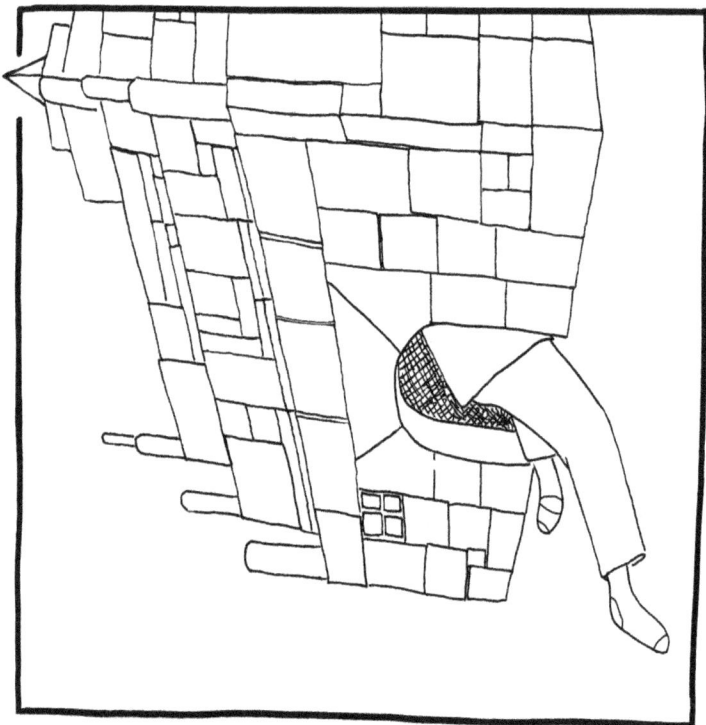

tip

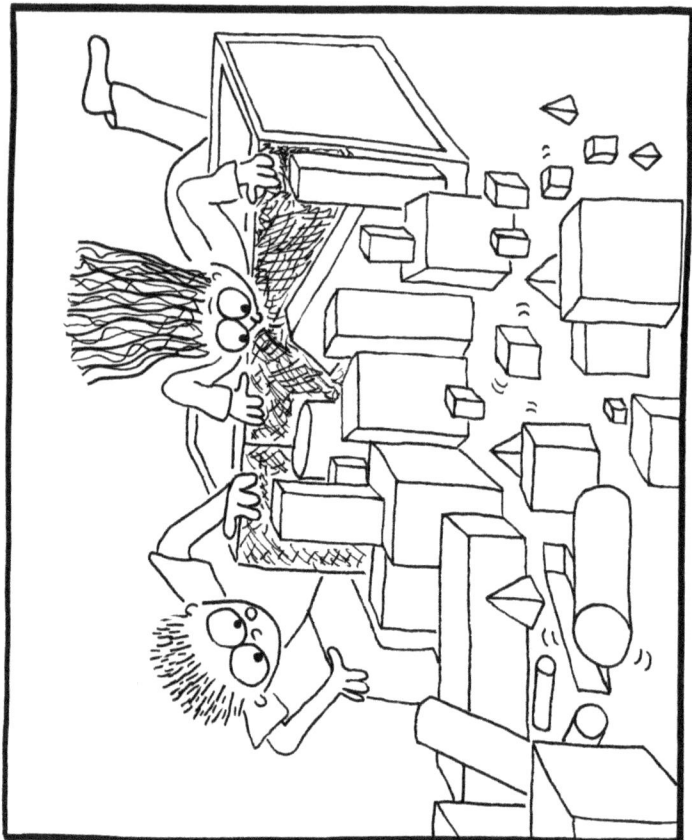

in

2

q

cut

3

cut

tip

3

big

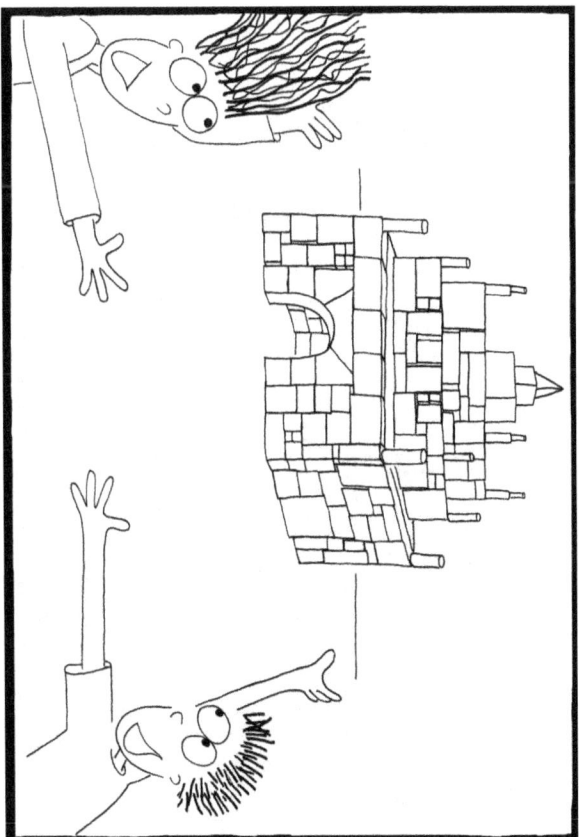

8

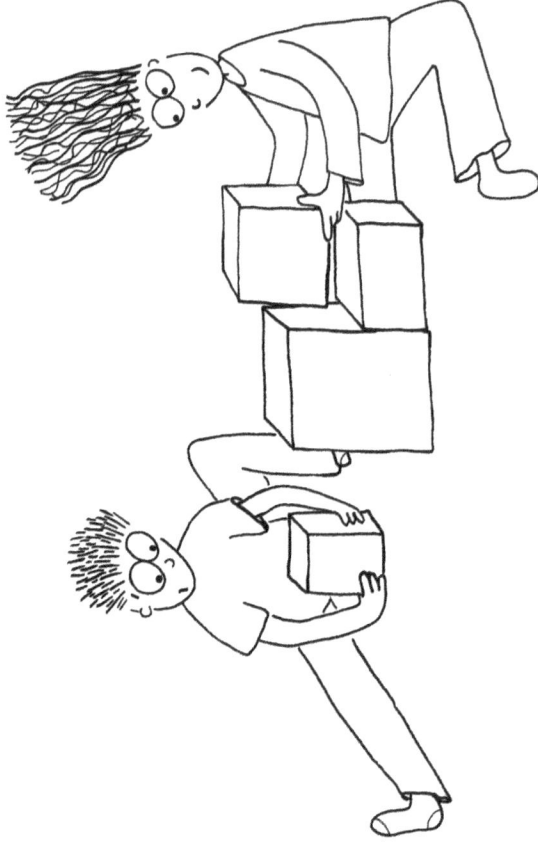

sit

4

fix

7

SET 2.2 – Book 3 – GUMDROPS FOR MOPPET TOPS

5

cut

big

fit

6

DOC

DOC

Mom jot
Tom box
hot pop
Doc

Got it!

Story and Pictures by Mark Linley

GUMDROPS for MOPPET TOPS SET 2.2

bartlebysbox.com

cut

cut

I

Mom

I

Tom

10

bartlebysbox.com

Tom

2

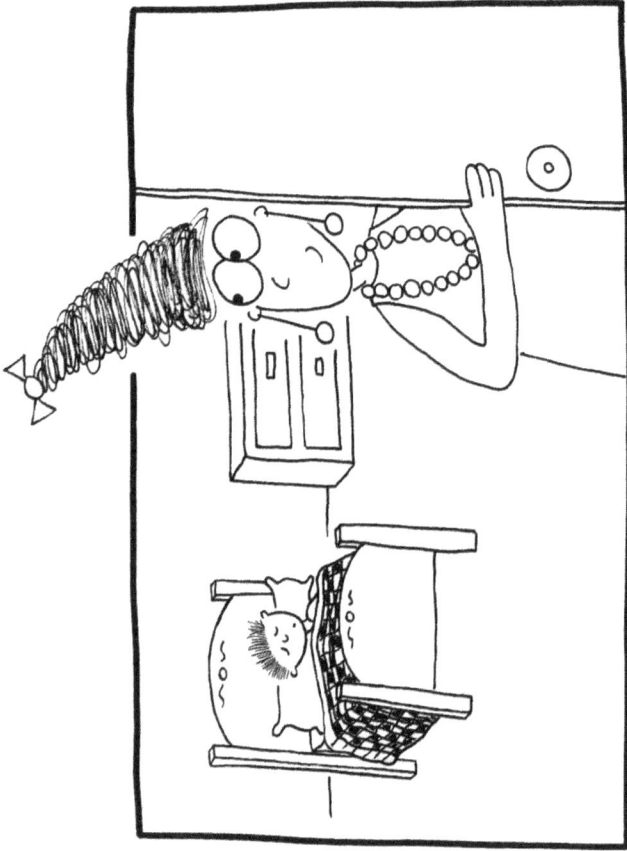

Mom

q

3

cut

hot

pop

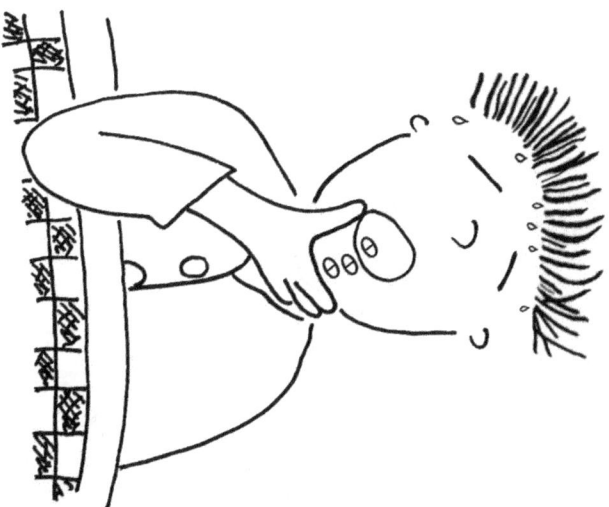

8

Doc

4

box

7

cut

5

cut

hot

jot

6

RUN

Story and Pictures by Mark Linley

SET 2.2

RUN

run fun
bus up
sub hug
rug

Got it!

bartlebysbox.com

cut

3

cut

run

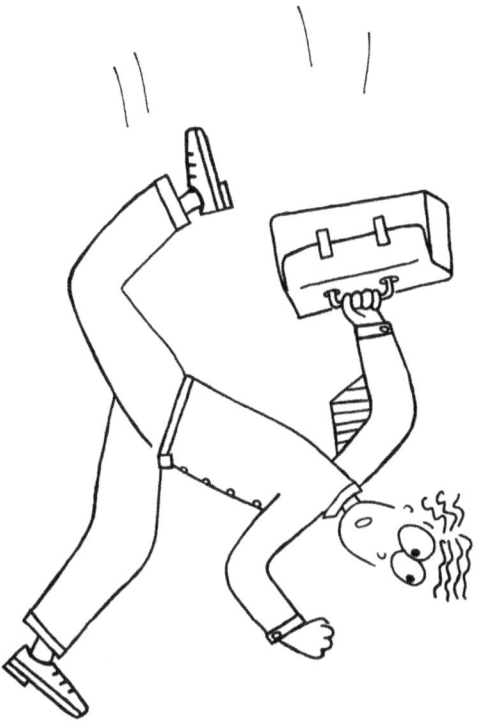

fun

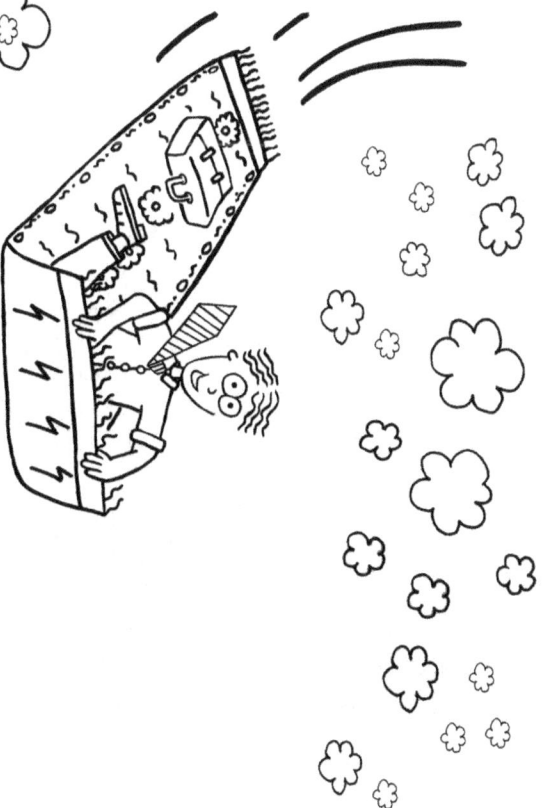

8

bartlebysbox.com

sub

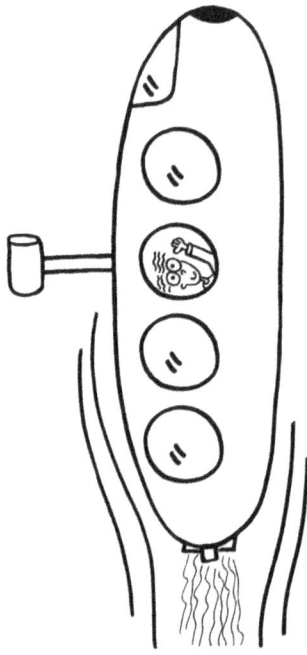

rug

cut

5

cut

run

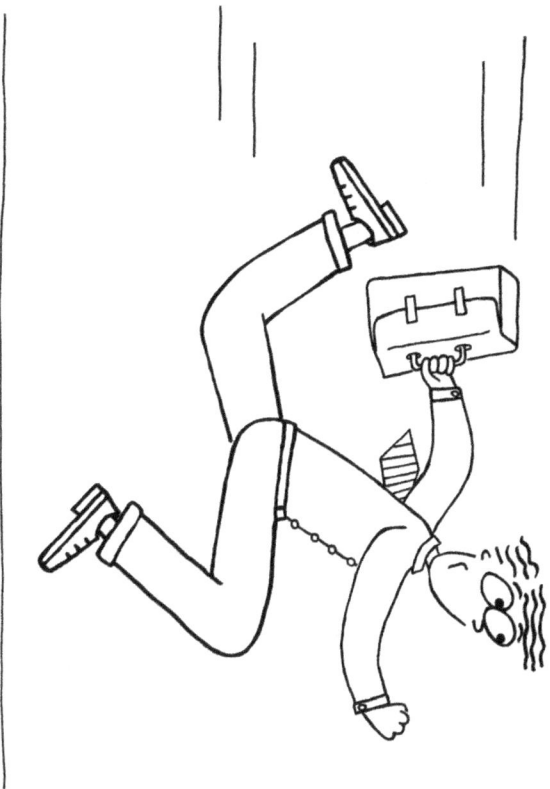

6

run

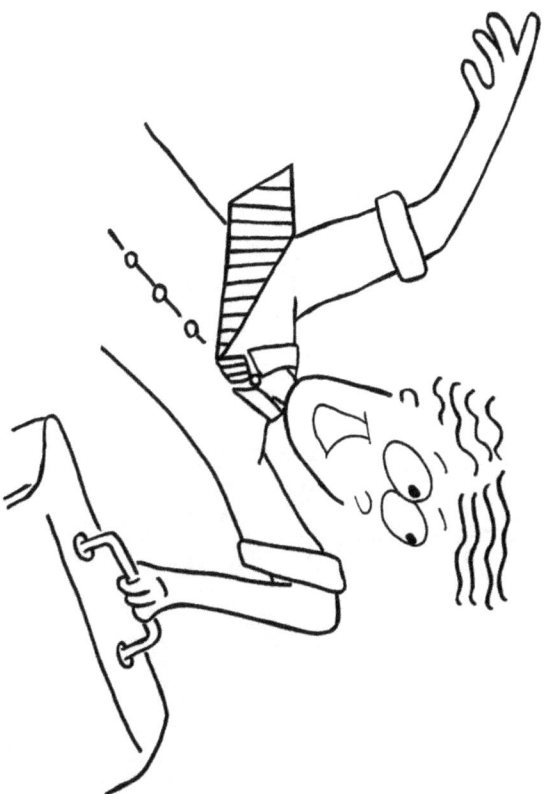

BAM !

cap ran
bat tag
fan sad
bam pal

Got it!

BAM !

Story and Pictures by Mark Linley

SET 2.3

GUMDROPS for MOPPET TOPS

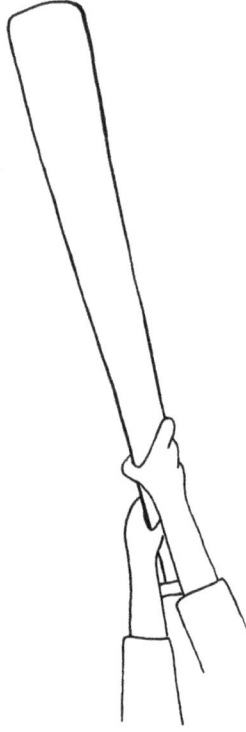

bartlebysbox.com

cut

I

cut

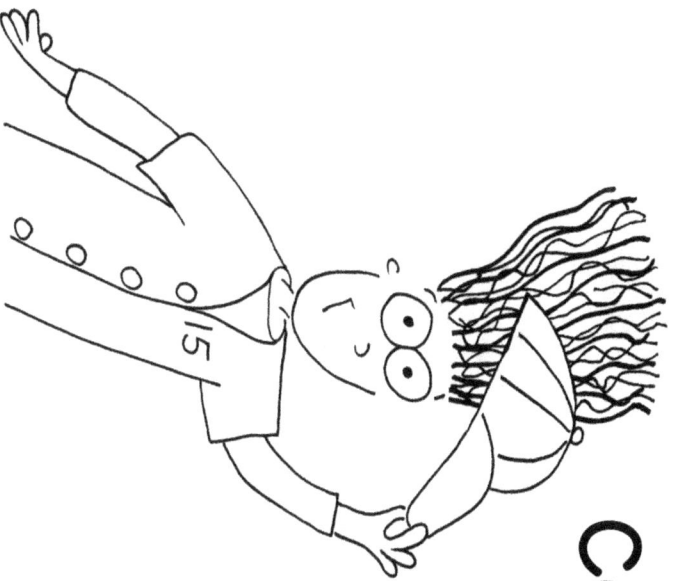

cap

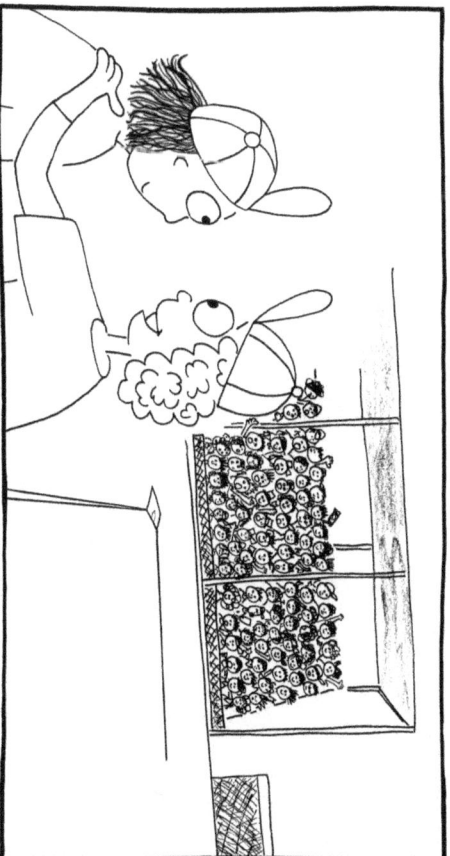

pal

I

10

bartlebysbox.com

bat

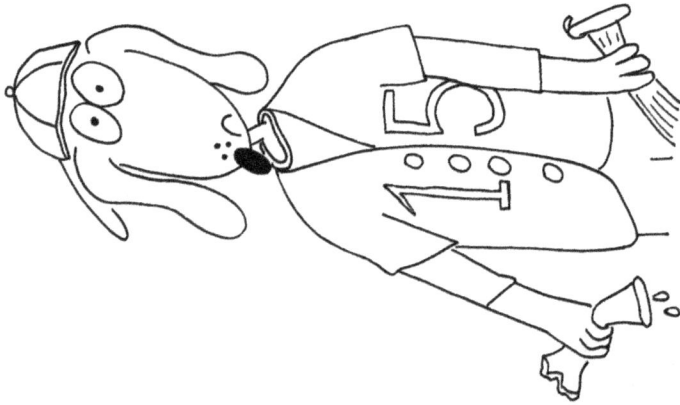

sad

SET 2.3 - Book 1 - GUMDROPS FOR MOPPET TOPS

3

cut

fan

8

tag

bartlebysbox.com

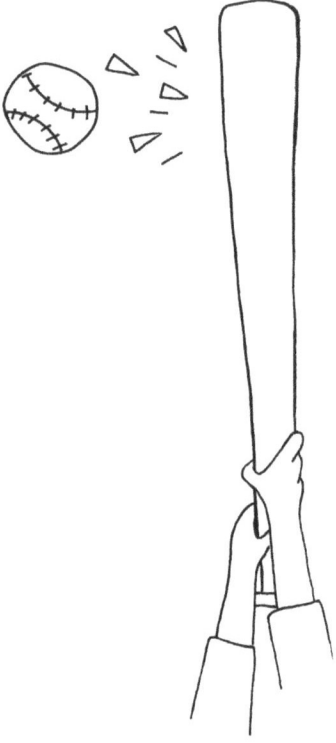

BAM

4

ran

7

cut

5

cut

ran

5

6

fan

VET

Rex   men
beg   leg
get   vet
yes   bed

Got it!

Story and Pictures by Mark Linley

VET

GUMDROPS for MOPPET TOPS

SET 2.3

bartlebysbox.com

cut

cut

I

Rex

bed

10

bartlebysbox.com

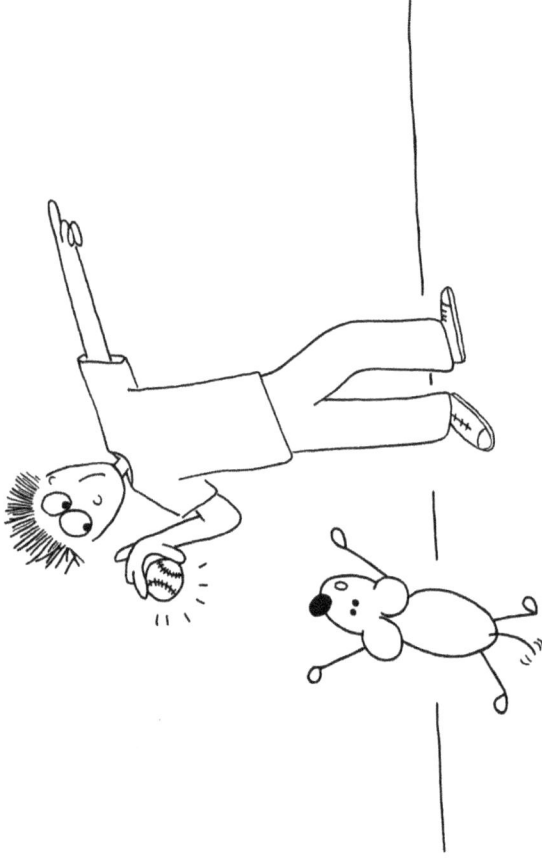

beg

2

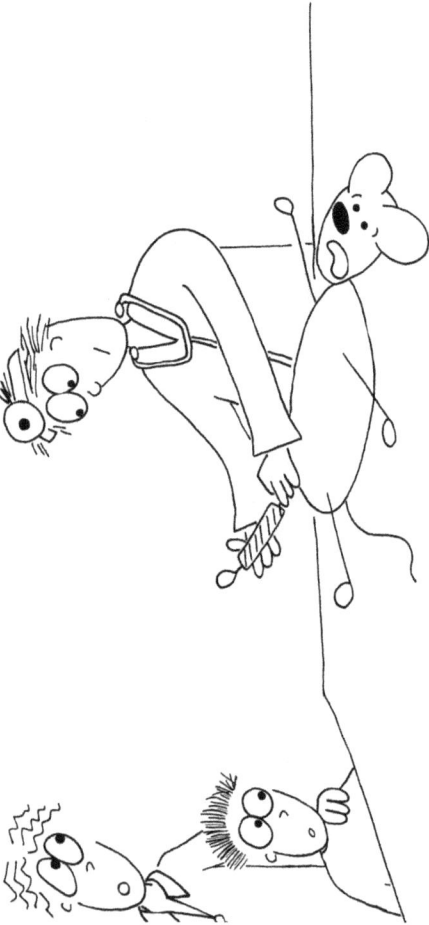

vet

q

cut

SET 2.3 – Book 2 – GUMDROPS FOR MOPPET TOPS

3

cut

get

3

get

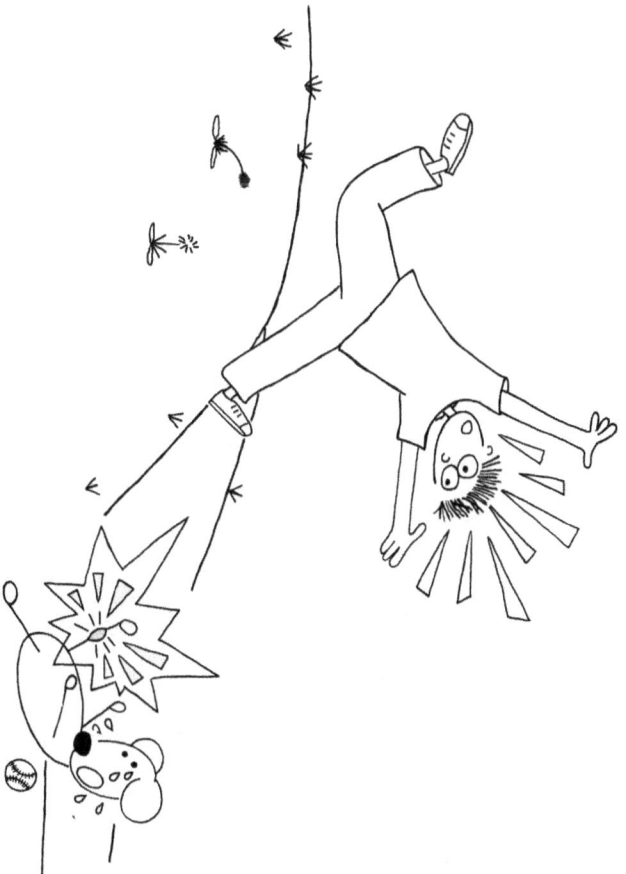

8

Rex

4

leg

7

cut

SET 2.3 - Book 2 - GUMDROPS FOR MOPPET TOPS

5

cut

yes

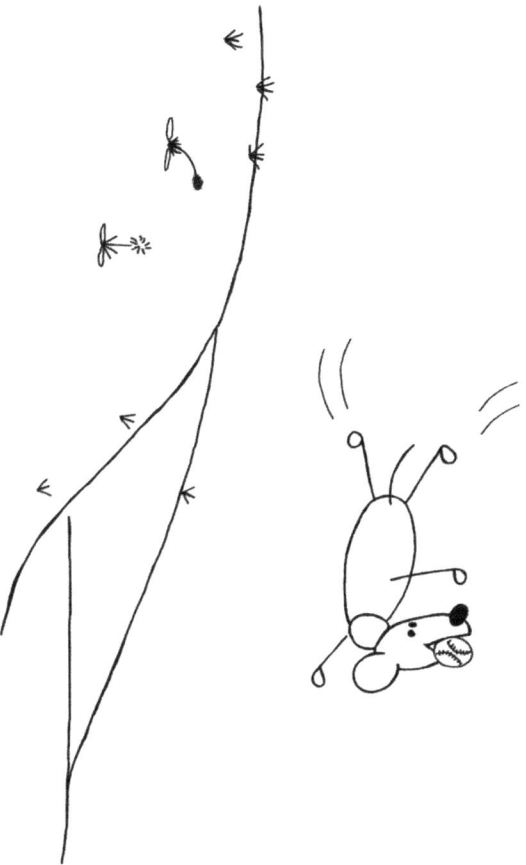

men

6

PIG SIPS

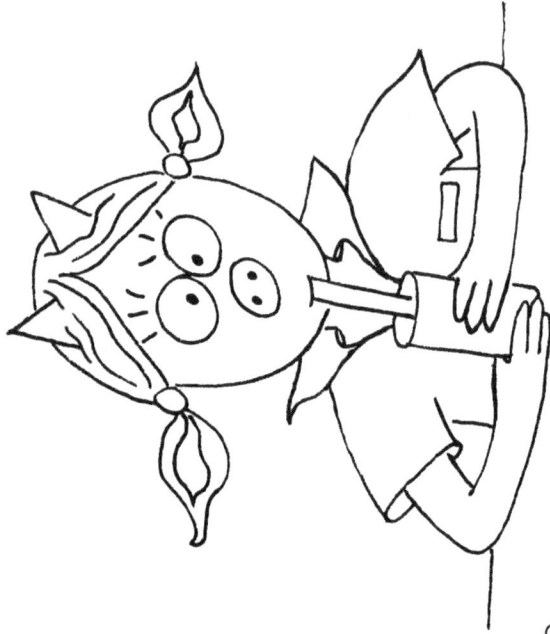

Story and Pictures by Mark Linley

SET 2.3

GUMDROPS for MOPPET TOPS

Got it!

PIG SIPS

mix
sip
tip

pig
zip
in
sit

bartlebysbox.com

cut

cut

I —

pig

tip

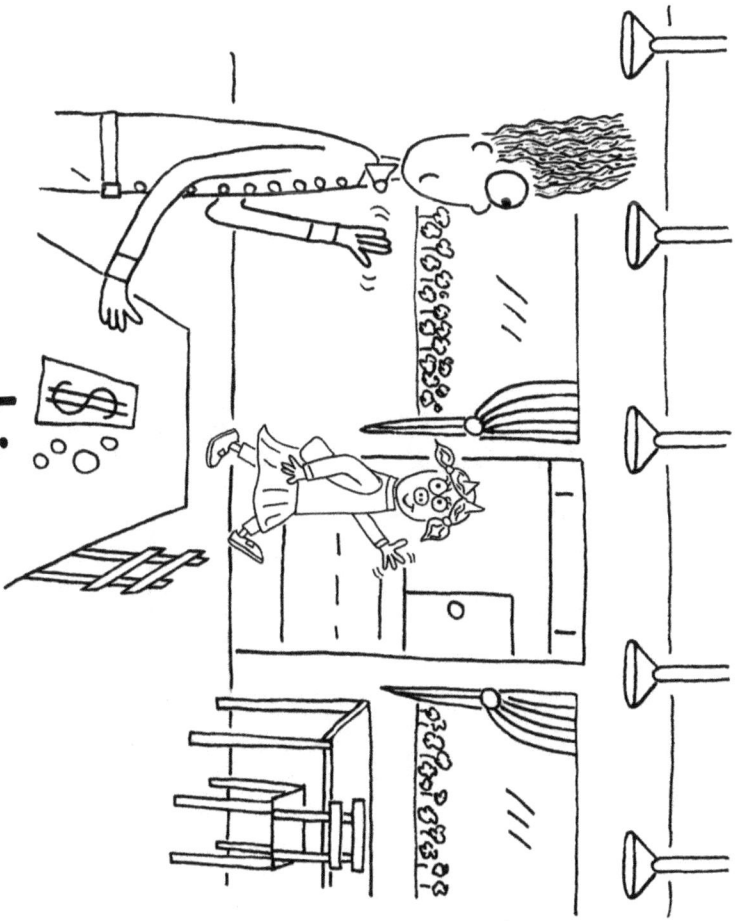

I —

IO

2

zip

q   cut

sip

SET 2.3 - Book 3 - GUMDROPS FOR MOPPET TOPS

3

cut

in

sip

3

8

in

4

pig

7

cut

5

cut

sit

6

mix

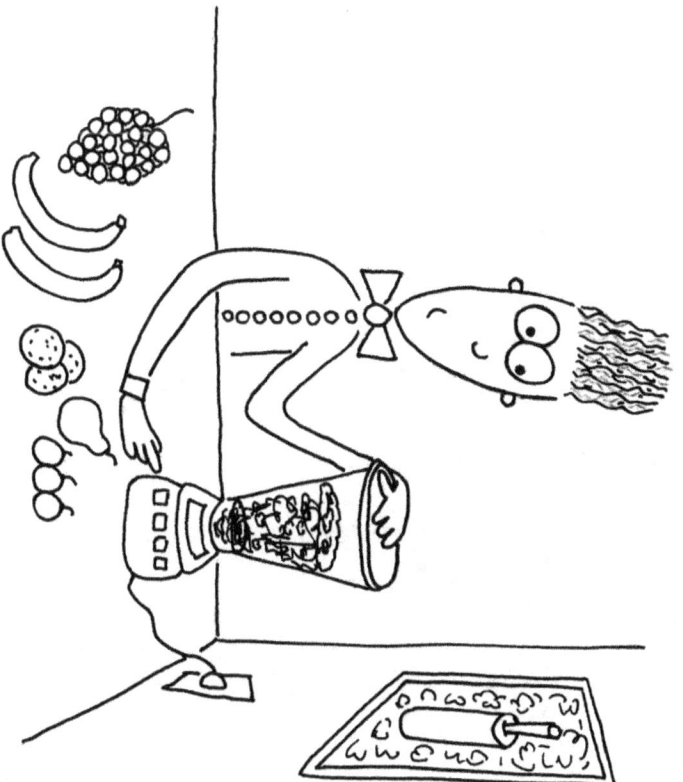

bartlebysbox.com

TOP DOG

Story and Pictures by Mark Linley

GUMDROPS for MOPPET TOPS

SET 2.3

TOP DOG

dog   hop

job   hot

on

Got it!

bartlebysbox.com

cut

I

cut

dog

dog

10

job

hot

q

cut

SET 2.3 – Book 4 – GUMDROPS FOR MOPPET TOPS

cut

3

on

3

dog

8

hop

4

cut

hop

7

cut

5

dog

5

6

hop

FUN FUN FUN FUN

FUN FUN FUN

up   sub
hug   tub
yum   bus
fun   us

Got it!

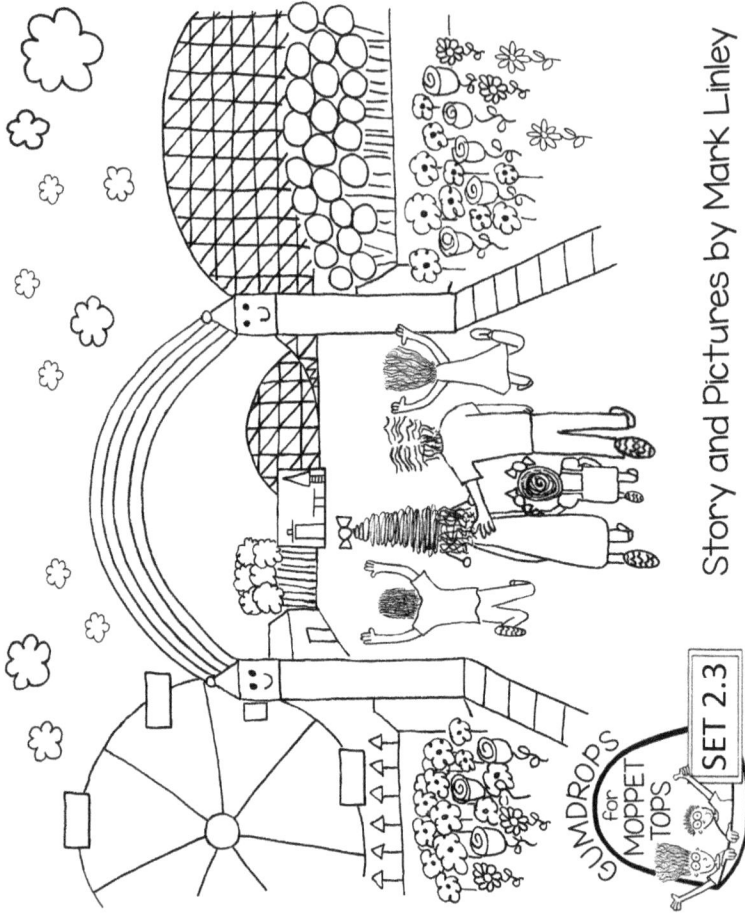

Story and Pictures by Mark Linley

SET 2.3

GUMDROPS for MOPPET TOPS

bartlebysbox.com

cut

cut

I

up

10

us

hug

2

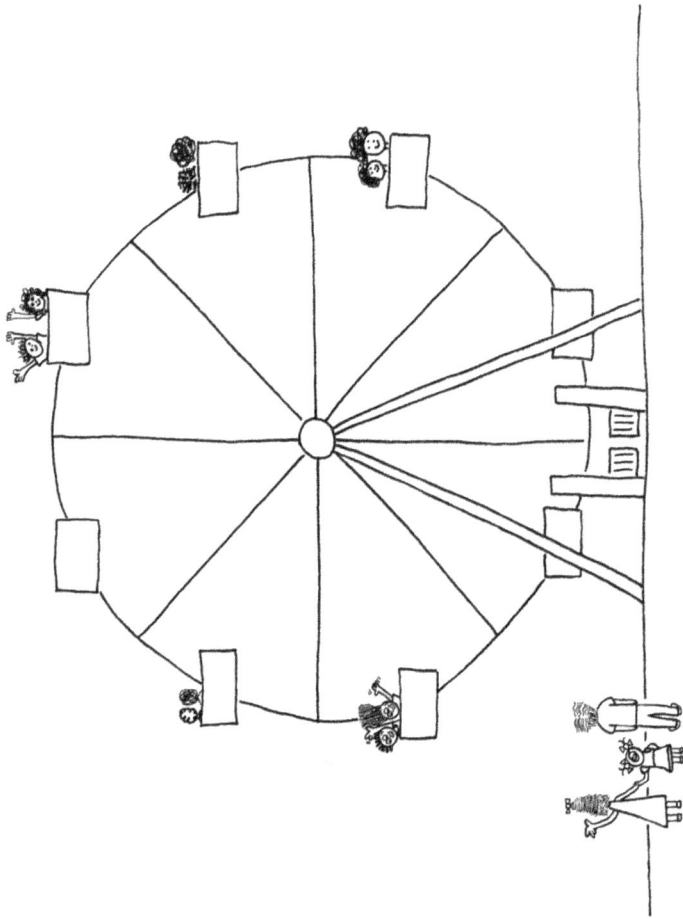

up

b

cut

SET 2.3 - Book 5 - GUMDROPS FOR MOPPET TOPS

3

cut

yum

8

fun

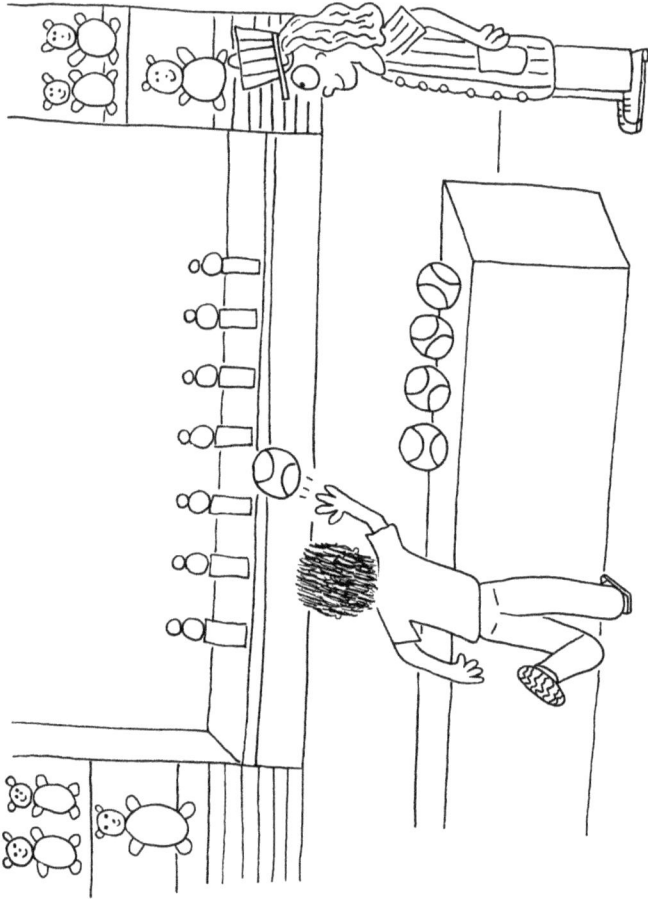

fun

4

bus

7

cut

5

cut

sub

5   6

tub

bartlebysbox.com

LESSON PLANS

Sequence of Instruction

Provided here is a suggested Lesson Plan for teaching CVC decoding in tandem with reading comprehension.

OPENING QUESTIONS

Ask one or more questions from **BEFORE READING** (See **Comprehension Questions**, following)

INTRODUCE the CVC WORDS

PREVIEW the book's CVC words on the board (Use the Back Cover of the book for a list of words)

> *Procedure for Demonstrating Blending, Sound by Sound*
> 1. Write one CVC word from the book on the board
>   Point to each letter and enunciate the sound of each letter: /c/ - /a/ - /t/
>   Point to the first two letters and enunciate the first two phonemes, then
>   the final consonant: /ca/ - /t/. *Or,* point to the first letter and
>   enunciate the first phoneme, then the medial vowel and final consonant:
>   /c/ - /at/
>   Swipe your finger under the word and blend the entire word: 'cat'
> 2. Repeat the above sequence as your students chorally read along with you
> 3. Write the next word, and so on....

READ TOGETHER

GIVE students their own copies of the book
READ each page

> For each page, consider doing the following:
> 1. ENCOURAGE students to look at the picture and make comments
> 2. ASK questions from **DURING READING** (See **Comprehension Questions**, following)
> 3. DECODE the page's word
>   Teacher: *Put your finger under the first letter. Ready begin.*
>   Teacher and students: /c/ - /a/ - /t/, /ca/ - /t/
>   or /c/ - /a/ - /t/, /c/ - /at/
>   Teacher: *What's the word?*
>   Teacher and students: *'cat'*

CONTINUE reading the entire book

CLOSING

DIRECT students to read the words on the Back Cover independently
ASK questions from **AFTER READING** (See **Comprehension Questions**, following)
ASSIGN further study
    Students re-read the book
    Students retell the story to a friend
    Students follow up with GUMDROPS for MOPPET TOPS Independent Practice Worksheets
    Students spell the words with their own letter cards (sets of letters can be made with
        marker on index cards)
    Students write the words
    Students color the books
    Students take the books home to read with family

Comprehension Questions

Provided here are a variety of questions to ask your students BEFORE, DURING, and AFTER they read. Some teachers may ask many or all of the questions, some teachers only a few. Often one question alone will yeild a rich and lengthy discussion. Many of these questions can be used as writing prompts as well. Of course, a teacher may decide to ask no comprehension questions at all, making their lesson a strictly phonics one.

SET 2.1 - Book 1

TAG

BEFORE READING

What games do you like to play outside?

Do you play tag? Do you like to play tag? Why? Why not?

What are the rules of the game of tag? Do kids sometimes make up different rules? What are they?

DURING READING

Title Page	When you play tag, do you like to be 'it'? Why? Why not? In your opinion, what is good about being 'it'? What is bad about being 'it'?
Page 1	What is happening here? How many kids are playing?
Page 2	What is the girl doing? What is she thinking?
Page 3	What is this girl doing? What is she saying? Do kids like to taunt or tease the person who is "it"? What do they say? What do they do?
Page 4	What is this boy doing?
Page 5	What is happening here?
Page 6	What is happening here? What will happen next?
Page 7	What is Cat thinking?
Page 8	What happened to the boy's cap? What will happen now?
Page 9	What is the girl thinking?
Page 10	What happened? Is this what you thought would happen? What might happen next in the story?

AFTER READING

What did you think about as you read this book?

Do you think these kids play fair?

If one of these kids was not playing fairly, what should the other kids do? What should they say?

If there are kids at your school or in your neighborhood that you want to play with, what do you do? How do you make new friends? How do you keep the friends you already have? How should you treat your friends?

Comprehension Questions

Provided here are a variety of questions to ask your students BEFORE, DURING, and AFTER they read. Some teachers may ask many or all of the questions, some teachers only a few. Often one question alone will yeild a rich and lengthy discussion. Many of these questions can be used as writing prompts as well. Of course, a teacher may decide to ask no comprehension questions at all, making their lesson a strictly phonics one.

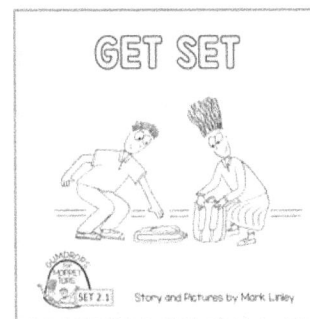

GET SET

BEFORE READING

What do you do when you wake up?

What do you have to do each morning to get ready for the day? What do you do first when you wake up? What do you do next? And then? And then?

Do you rush in the morning? Who in your family is the first to get ready? Who is the slowest?

Who in your family helps others to get ready? How do they help them? How do you help?

DURING READING

Title Page	What do you think this book is about? What are the kids doing?
Page 1	What time of day is it? How do you know?
Page 2	Do you like to take baths? Do you ever take baths in the morning? Do you like bubble baths? Do you play with toys in the bath? What do you pretend?
Page 3	Is it easy for you to get out of bed or is it difficult? Do you parents have to help you get up or can you get up all by yourself? Do you wake up before your parents?
Page 4	Do you like to take showers? What do you like about showers? Do you prefer showers or baths? Why?
Page 5	What is happening here? Can you get your breakfast by yourself? Do you like to do things all by yourself? Does someone make breakfast for you?
Page 6	What is this boy having for breakfast? What do you eat for breakfast?
Page 7	After you eat, do you clean up after yourself or does someone clean up after you?
Page 8	Can you brush your teeth all by yourself? Do you have any cavities? Why is it important to brush your teeth? Do you floss? Why is flossing important? What would a dentist say?
Page 9	Do you have a backpack? Why do kids bring backpacks to school? What do you like to keep in your backpack? Is there anything that you would like to keep in your backpack, but you can't because you are not allowed?
Page 10	What is happening here? How do these kids get to school? Have you ever ridden on a bus? How do you get to school?

AFTER READING

What did this story make you think about?

Is your morning routine different from the kids' routine in this book? How is it different? How is it the same?

Does your morning routine change on weekends? Does it change if you go on vacation?

Why do people go to school? What do you like about school? What would you change about school if you could?

Comprehension Questions

Provided here are a variety of questions to ask your students BEFORE, DURING, and AFTER they read. Some teachers may ask many or all of the questions, some teachers only a few. Often one question alone will yeild a rich and lengthy discussion. Many of these questions can be used as writing prompts as well. Of course, a teacher may decide to ask no comprehension questions at all, making their lesson a strictly phonics one.

PIG IS IN

BEFORE READING

Have you ever been in a pool? a lake? a river? an ocean?

Do you know how to swim? Can you float? Can you keep your head above water without a floatie or a raft?

Or do you wade and splash around only?

Do you like to go swimming?

What kinds of fun do you have when you are in the water? What do you play?

What do other people do in the water?

DURING READING

Title Page	What is Pig doing?
Page 1	If you could talk to Pig, what would you say to her?
Page 2	What might Pig say to you?
Page 3	What do you like to drink on a hot day? What might Pig be thinking about?
Page 4	What do you think Pig has in the bag?
Page 5	What is Pig looking for? What kinds of things might be in a bag to bring to a pool?
Page 6	What did Pig find? What is Pig doing? Why do people wear fins or flippers in the water? How do fins or flippers help a swimmer?
Page 7	What happened? Have you ever ripped clothing of yours? Was it fixed? Does anyone on your family know how to sew?
Page 8	How did Pig fix her ripped wetsuit? Is this a permanent fix, or will she have to repair it further?
Page 9	What is Pig wearing on her eyes? Why does she wear goggles? Do you know how to dive?
Page 10	What will Pig do now in the pool? Do you think Pig knows how to swim? How do you know she does?

AFTER READING

How much time passes in this story?

How did this story begin? What happened next? Then what happened? How did the story end?

If you could talk to Pig, what would you say to her? What would she say to you? What would you do together?

What if you could jump in a pool right now? What would you like to do in the water? What games would you play?

What does this story make you think about?

Comprehension Questions

Provided here are a variety of questions to ask your students BEFORE, DURING, and AFTER they read. Some teachers may ask many or all of the questions, some teachers only a few. Often one question alone will yeild a rich and lengthy discussion. Many of these questions can be used as writing prompts as well. Of course, a teacher may decide to ask no comprehension questions at all, making their lesson a strictly phonics one.

POP

BEFORE READING

What snacks do you like to eat?

Do you eat snacks at home that are different than snacks you eat at school?

Do you eat different snacks when you go out with your parents?

Do you eat different snacks when you go over to other people's houses?

Have you ever made popcorn? How is popcorn made?

DURING READING

Title Page	What is the title of this story? What do you think this story is about?
Page 1	Who is this? What is his name? Where is he standing? How old do you think he is?
Page 2	Who is this? What is her name? Where is she standing? How old is she?
Page 3	Who is this? What is her name? What is in her mouth? How old is she?
Page 4	Who is this? Where is she standing? What is her name? Do you think that Mom has another name, a first name? What is your mom's first name? What is your dad's first name?
Page 5	What is Mom holding? What is in the pot?
Page 6	What is happening to the pot?
Page 7	What just popped? (An air bubble inside the kernal expanded with the heat and the corn exploded)
Page 8	Now what is happening? Have you ever heard popcorn pop?
Page 9	How does Mom feel? Why does she feel this way?
Page 10	How do the kids feel? Why? If you could speak to these kids, what would you say to them? What might they say to you?

AFTER READING

The dad does not appear in this story. Where might the dad be?

What is your favorite snack to eat at home?

Why is it important to spend time with your family?

Why is it important to share? How do you feel when you share something of yours with someone else? How do you feel when someone shares with you?

Do you share snacks with your family?

Comprehension Questions

SET 2.1 - Book 5

Provided here are a variety of questions to ask your students BEFORE, DURING, and AFTER they read. Some teachers may ask many or all of the questions, some teachers only a few. Often one question alone will yeild a rich and lengthy discussion. Many of these questions can be used as writing prompts as well. Of course, a teacher may decide to ask no comprehension questions at all, making their lesson a strictly phonics one.

SUN FUN

BEFORE READING

> Do you like to play outside? What do you do? What do you like to play?
>
> Do you ever play outside alone? Do you play outside with friends? Would you rather play alone or with friends?
>
> Do you like to go to the park? Who do you go with? What do you do at the park?

DURING READING

Title Page	What is Dog doing?
Page 1	If Dog could speak to you, what would he say? What would you say to him?
Page 2	Do you think Dog is being safe? Do you like to climb trees? Do your parents like you to climb trees? Do they let you climb trees?
Page 3	Why did Dog run?
Page 4	Do you like this play structure? If you were on it, what would you do?
Page 5	Do you ever go down a slide head-first?
Page 6	Do you like to go on swings? Do you know how to pump? Do you like to have someone push you? Have you ever jumped off of a swing?
Page 7	Now why is Dog running?
Page 8	Do you like to play basketball? Have you ever made a basket? If you could be a superstar in any sport when you grow up, what sport would you choose? Why?
Page 9	Now what is Dog doing? What is he thinking?
Page 10	What do you think Dog will do next?

AFTER READING

> What did you think about as you read this book?
>
> What is Dog like? Would you like to be his friend?
>
> If you could go to the park and meet Dog, what would you do together?
>
> When you go to the park, do you make new friends with kids you don't know?
>
> How do you become friends with someone that you do not yet know? What do you do? What do you say?

Comprehension Questions

Provided here are a variety of questions to ask your students BEFORE, DURING, and AFTER they read. Some teachers may ask many or all of the questions, some teachers only a few. Often one question alone will yeild a rich and lengthy discussion. Many of these questions can be used as writing prompts as well. Of course, a teacher may decide to ask no comprehension questions at all, making their lesson a strictly phonics one.

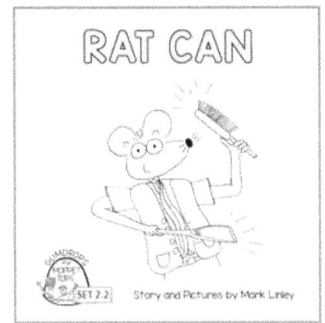

RAT CAN

BEFORE READING

Do you help your family keep your house clean?
What do you do to help? What more can you do to help?
Why is it important to keep your house clean?
What tools and products do people use to keep their houses clean?

DURING READING

Title Page	What is rat holding? What is a dustpan and brush used for? What do you think this story will be about?
Page 1	What is Rat doing? Do you know how to use a broom? What are brooms used for?
Page 2	Have you ever used a dustpan and brush? Why did you use them?
Page 3	How is a rag used for cleaning?
Page 4	Now what is Rat doing? What is he holding in his hand?
Page 5	Why does Rat need to get water?
Page 6	What is Rat thinking about?
Page 7	Now what is Rat using to clean? What is a mop used for? How does a mop work?
Page 8	How is Rat using the rag now? What is he cleaning?
Page 9	What is Rat doing now?
Page 10	Why is Rat sitting down? How does Rat feel? What is he thinking? Do you think Rat likes his home? Why do you think that?

AFTER READING

What does this story make you think about?
Do you think cleaning the house is hard work? Does it take a long time to do?
Who does most of the cleaning in your home? Is that fair? What are the other members of your family doing while this person is cleaning? Are they working too? What are you doing while others are cleaning?

Comprehension Questions

Provided here are a variety of questions to ask your students BEFORE, DURING, and AFTER they read. Some teachers may ask many or all of the questions, some teachers only a few. Often one question alone will yeild a rich and lengthy discussion. Many of these questions can be used as writing prompts as well. Of course, a teacher may decide to ask no comprehension questions at all, making their lesson a strictly phonics one.

JET

BEFORE READING

Do you dream at night? Do you remember your dreams?

Did you have a dream last night?

Do you remember any dreams you've had in the past?

Have you had dreams that you feel are really important to you?

Do you have dreams that repeat themselves on different nights?

DURING READING

Title Page	Have you ever been on a plane before? Where did you go? What happened?
Page 1	What kind of hat is dog wearing? (It's a nightcap)
Page 2	Do you wear pajamas or a nightgown? Do you have a favorite blanket or pillow at home? What does it look like?
Page 3	What is happening? What is Dog dreaming of?
Page 4	What is inside the plane? Do airplanes normally have beds like this? Do people sometimes sleep on planes?
Page 5	What is happening here?
Page 6	Have you ever had a dream about falling? How is Dog feeling?
Page 7	What are the men doing?
Page 8	How do you know that this is a dream?
Page 9	What happened?
Page 10	Is Dog still dreaming? What happened? What is Dog thinking? What will he do next?

AFTER READING

How do Dog's feelings change in this story?

When you wake up from a bad dream, how do you feel? What do you think about? What do you do?

Do you tell someone about your dreams, or do you keep them to yourself?

Do you have scary dreams? Do you have happy dreams?

Would you like to talk about a dream you've had?

Comprehension Questions

Provided here are a variety of questions to ask your students BEFORE, DURING, and AFTER they read. Some teachers may ask many or all of the questions, some teachers only a few. Often one question alone will yeild a rich and lengthy discussion. Many of these questions can be used as writing prompts as well. Of course, a teacher may decide to ask no comprehension questions at all, making their lesson a strictly phonics one.

SET 2.2 - Book 3

KIDS

BEFORE READING

Do you like to play with blocks? What do you do with the blocks?
What do you build? Do you bring dolls or other toys into your block-play?
Do you like to play alone or with somebody else?
What do you like to play? What do you pretend when you play with blocks?

DURING READING

Title Page	What does this front cover make you think of? Would you like to play with these blocks? What would you build?
Page 1	What are the kids doing?
Page 2	What do you think happened here? What do you think of these blocks? What shapes do you see? (cubes, prisms, pyramids, cylinders)
Page 3	Have you ever built a tower of blocks? Did it tip over?
Page 4	Now what are the kids doing?
Page 5	Have you ever used such large blocks? Do you think these blocks are heavy?
Page 6	What do you think they are trying to build?
Page 7	What is the girl doing?
Page 8	What did the kids build?
Page 9	What is happening here?
Page 10	Now what will they do? What might they play? What story might they act out?

AFTER READING

Have you ever been in a playhouse? How do kids play in playhouses? What do they do?
Have you ever played in a treehouse or found a great hiding place?
Have you ever made an indoor fort with a blanket? Have you ever used an indoor play-tent or play-castle?
What games did you play? What stories did you act out? What did you pretend?
Do you like to pretend?

Comprehension Questions

Provided here are a variety of questions to ask your students BEFORE, DURING, and AFTER they read. Some teachers may ask many or all of the questions, some teachers only a few. Often one question alone will yeild a rich and lengthy discussion. Many of these questions can be used as writing prompts as well. Of course, a teacher may decide to ask no comprehension questions at all, making their lesson a strictly phonics one.

DOC

BEFORE READING

Have you ever been sick? What happened?
Has someone in your family ever been sick?
Have you ever been to see the doctor? Why did you go?
Have you ever been to the hospital? Why did you go?

DURING READING

Title Page	Who is this? What is her job? What do doctors do?
Page 1	How is the mom feeling? Does she look worried? Why would she be worried?
Page 2	What is the matter with Tom? Why is he sweating? Why is he crying?
Page 3	Why is Tom's mother touching his head this way? How is she feeling? What is she thinking?
Page 4	What questions might the doctor ask? What will the doctor do?
Page 5	What is happening here?
Page 6	What is the doctor writing? What does the word 'jot' mean?
Page 7	Why is Mom happy? What is in the box?
Page 8	Why is Tom taking pills? Have you ever taken pills? Have you ever taken medicine from a dropper, or mixed in a drink?
Page 9	How does Mom feel now? What is she thinking?
Page 10	How does Tom feel now?

AFTER READING

If you are sick, what do you have to do to help yourself get better?
What can you do to protect yourself from getting sick?
Mom worries about her son. Does your mom or dad (or other family member) worry about you?
What do they worry about? What do you worry about? What do you worry about most?

Comprehension Questions

Provided here are a variety of questions to ask your students BEFORE, DURING, and AFTER they read. Some teachers may ask many or all of the questions, some teachers only a few. Often one question alone will yeild a rich and lengthy discussion. Many of these questions can be used as writing prompts as well. Of course, a teacher may decide to ask no comprehension questions at all, making their lesson a strictly phonics one.

SET 2.2 - Book 5

RUN

BEFORE READING

Does your mom or dad work? Do they work at home or do they have to leave home to go to work?
If they leave home, how do they get to work? Do they go by bus, car, train, bike? Do they walk?
How do you feel when your mom or dad comes home?

DURING READING

Title Page	What do you think this book is about? What is the man holding? What might be in his bag?
Page 1	Where do you think the dad is going? Why is he running?
Page 2	Does your mom or dad take a bus to work? Have you ever ridden on a bus?
Page 3	Why is the dad running? What is he thinking?
Page 4	What kind of vehicle is this? Do you think many people take a submarine to work?
Page 5	Now why is he running? What do you think he running towards?
Page 6	How is he feeling now? What might happen next?
Page 7	What is this?
Page 8	Are flying carpets real? If you could fly on a magic carpet, where would you go? What would you do?
Page 9	Now do you know where the man is running?
Page 10	Why does the dad hurry to get home? How does the family feel when Dad gets home?

AFTER READING

How is this family similar to your family? How is the family different from yours?
Does your mom or dad have to travel far to get to work? Does it take them a long time to get home from work?
What do you think this dad's job is?
What do you want to be when you grow up?
What did you think about as you read this story?

Comprehension Questions

Provided here are a variety of questions to ask your students BEFORE, DURING, and AFTER they read. Some teachers may ask many or all of the questions, some teachers only a few. Often one question alone will yeild a rich and lengthy discussion. Many of these questions can be used as writing prompts as well. Of course, a teacher may decide to ask no comprehension questions at all, making their lesson a strictly phonics one.

SET 2.3 - Book 1

BAM!

BEFORE READING

> What sports do you like to play?
> What sport would you like to learn to play?
> Does anyone in your family play a sport? What sport?

DURING READING

Title Page	What sport is this book about? How do you know? Do you know anyone who plays baseball? Have you ever been to a baseball game?
Page 1	Why do baseball players wear caps? If you could say something to the girl, what would you say? What might she say to you?
Page 2	What is the girl thinking? What is she getting ready to do?
Page 3	Who is this? What is a fan?
Page 4	What happened?
Page 5	Why did the girl run?
Page 6	Why does the fan look so excited?
Page 7	What is happening here?
Page 8	What happened?
Page 9	Why does the fan look sad?
Page 10	How is the girl's friend a good friend? What is her friend doing? What is her friend saying? How does the girl feel?

AFTER READING

> If you could change this story to have a different ending, what would you change?
> If you lose a game or lose your turn, do you get sad or mad?
> If you feel bad about something, how do you make yourself feel better?
> Have you ever tried to make a friend feel better? What did you do?
> Is there a lesson or moral to be learned from this book?

Comprehension Questions

Provided here are a variety of questions to ask your students BEFORE, DURING, and AFTER they read. Some teachers may ask many or all of the questions, some teachers only a few. Often one question alone will yeild a rich and lengthy discussion. Many of these questions can be used as writing prompts as well. Of course, a teacher may decide to ask no comprehension questions at all, making their lesson a strictly phonics one.

VET

BEFORE READING

Why do people have pets? What kinds of pets do people have? Do you have a pet?

Do you, or does anyone you know, have a dog for a pet? Have you ever played with a dog? What did you do with the dog?

What do dogs like to do? What games do dogs like to play?

DURING READING

Title Page	What is a vet? What does a vet do in his or her job? What do you think is going to happen in this story?
Page 1	What is this dog's name?
Page 2	What is the boy doing? What is the dog doing? What is going to happen next?
Page 3	What is the name of the game that the boy and Rex are playing? Have you ever played fetch with a dog?
Page 4	Do you think Rex will catch the ball? Where will Rex land?
Page 5	Do you remember the title of this book? What does a vet have to do with what is happening in this in this book?
Page 6	What are the men doing? What are they thinking? What are they saying?
Page 7	What happened?
Page 8	What is the boy doing? What is he thinking? How is he feeling?
Page 9	Why is Rex now at the vet? What is the vet doing?
Page 10	How is the family feeling? How is Rex feeling?

AFTER READING

What was the problem in this story? How was it solved? What will happen next in the story?

Have you ever tried hard to do something and hurt yourself? What happened?

Have you ever been badly hurt? Has anyone you know been badly hurt? What happened?

What did you think about as you read this book? How did your feelings change as you read this book?

Comprehension Questions

Provided here are a variety of questions to ask your students BEFORE, DURING, and AFTER they read. Some teachers may ask many or all of the questions, some teachers only a few. Often one question alone will yeild a rich and lengthy discussion. Many of these questions can be used as writing prompts as well. Of course, a teacher may decide to ask no comprehension questions at all, making their lesson a strictly phonics one.

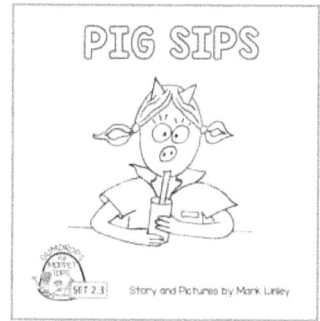

PIG SIPS

BEFORE READING

Do you ever go out to a cafe or to a restaurant for a snack? Do you ever go with your mom or dad to a coffee shop, an ice cream shop, or chocolate shop. Do you ever go out to get a fresh juice or a smoothie?

Does your family make fresh juice or smoothies at home? Do you know how smoothies are made? What has to be done first? What next? And after that?

DURING READING

Title Page	What is the title of this book? What is Pig doing? What might she be drinking?
Page 1	What is Pig thinking about?
Page 2	What is Pig doing? Why? What do you think will happen next?
Page 3	What is happening here?
Page 4	Where is Pig going? What kind of store is this? How do you know? What is on the sign above the door?
Page 5	What drink do you like to order when you go out? Do you like fruit? Do you have a favorite fruit? Do you have a favorite fruit drink?
Page 6	What is this man doing? What is his job?
Page 7	Do you like to use straws for drinking? Why do kids like straws?
Page 8	What is Pig thinking about?
Page 9	Does Pig like her drink? How do you know?
Page 10	What is happening here? What might Pig do next? Where might she go? What is a tip? Why do customers leave tips?

AFTER READING

What does this story make you think about?

If you could join Pig, what would you order? What would you talk about? What would you say to her? What might she say to you?

Does this story remind you of anything in your life? Does Pig remind you of anyone you know? How so?

Are fruit smoothies healthy to drink? If you had a choice, would you choose a fruit smoothie or a soda to drink?

Comprehension Questions

Provided here are a variety of questions to ask your students BEFORE, DURING, and AFTER they read. Some teachers may ask many or all of the questions, some teachers only a few. Often one question alone will yeild a rich and lengthy discussion. Many of these questions can be used as writing prompts as well. Of course, a teacher may decide to ask no comprehension questions at all, making their lesson a strictly phonics one.

TOP DOG

BEFORE READING

Can you ride a bike? Can you ride a scooter? Can you skate?

Which of these would you like to learn? Is there another sport you would like to learn?

Have you ever been to an extreme sporting event? (BMX biking, mountain biking, skateboarding, surfing, rock climbing, white water rafting, snowboarding, skiing…)

Have you ever seen videos of extreme sports? Do you know anyone who does an extreme sport?

DURING READING

Title Page	What is Dog doing on his bicycle? What does the word 'hot' mean in this title? What might this story be about?
Page 1	If you were riding a bike, what would you do? Where would you go? Why?
Page 2	What is Dog doing? What might have happened?
Page 3	What is happening here?
Page 4	Do you know anyone who can do a jump on a bicycle? What other tricks do people do on bicycles? (Wheelie, slide, endo, bunnyhop, pogo, bar spin, one-handed, drop-off, nose wheelie...)
Page 5	This trick is called a 'one-handed hang-five jump'. Why is it called 'one handed'? Why is it called 'hang-five'? ('Hang-five' means one foot is off the pedal)
Page 6	This trick is called a 'one-handed hang-five inverted tabletop' (a 'tabletop' is the bike positioned flat, parallel to the ground; 'inverted' means than the bike is moved further than the tabletop to be almost upside down)
Page 7	This trick is called a 'cross-up' with a 'tabletop' (in a 'cross up' the front wheel is turned 90 degrees or more)
Page 8	What does the word 'hot' mean here?
Page 9	This trick is a 'one-handed flip' with a 'tail-whip' (tail-whip is the rear wheel moving sideways)
Page 10	What would your parents think if you could do tricks like these?

AFTER READING

What did you think about as you read this book?

Why is it important to wear a helmet? For what other sports do you have to wear a helmet? (Ice skating, skates, scootering, sky diving….)

If you could talk to Dog, what would you ask him? What would you say? What would Dog say to you?

Comprehension Questions

Provided here are a variety of questions to ask your students BEFORE, DURING, and AFTER they read. Some teachers may ask many or all of the questions, some teachers only a few. Often one question alone will yeild a rich and lengthy discussion. Many of these questions can be used as writing prompts as well. Of course, a teacher may decide to ask no comprehension questions at all, making their lesson a strictly phonics one.

FUN FUN FUN

BEFORE READING

Have you ever been to a fair or an amusement park? Who did you go with? What did you do?

What kinds of games, rides and activities do fairs and amusement parks have?

What else can you find at a fair or amusement park?

DURING READING

Title Page	Where is the family going? Is this a place where you would like to go?
Page 1	What kind of ride is this? Have you ever been on a roller coaster? How did it make you feel?
Page 2	How is the girl feeling? How is the mom feeling? And the boy?
Page 3	Have you ever eaten cotton candy? Can you describe it? What does it look like, feel like, smell like, taste like?
Page 4	What is the boy trying to do? What must he do to win? What happens if he wins?
Page 5	What is each character thinking? What do you like to eat for lunch?
Page 6	What is happening here? Have you ever used a dunk tank? Would you rather throw the ball or be dunked?
Page 7	Do you like merry-go-rounds? Does the girl? What is fun about a merry-go-round?
Page 8	Have you ever been on bumper cars? What happens?
Page 9	Have you ever been on a Ferris wheel?
Page 10	How does each character feel now? What are they thinking? What will they do next?

AFTER READING

What was this story about? Can you summarize this story?

How much time passes in this story?

What does this story make you think about?

Do you like to go places with your parents? Where do you like to go?

Why is it important to go places with your family?

INDEPENDENT PRACTICE WORKSHEETS

 TAG

NAME

DIRECTIONS: Retell the story, trace and write the words.

TRACE   WRITE

1.
   tag

2.
   ran

3.
   tag

4.
   tag

5.
   ran

 bartlebysbox.com

TAG

NAME

DIRECTIONS: Retell the story, trace and write the words.

TRACE   WRITE

6.

cat

7.

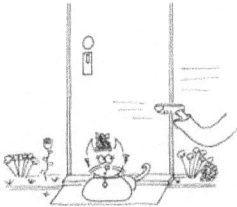
ran

8.

cap

9.

ran

10.

tag

SET 2.1 - Book 1
GUMDROPS FOR MOPPET TOPS

bartlebysbox.com

GET SET

NAME

DIRECTIONS: Retell the story, trace and write the words.

TRACE   WRITE

1.

bed

2.

wet

3.

bed

4.

wet

5.

set

bartlebysbox.com

GET SET

NAME

DIRECTIONS: Retell the story, trace and write the words.

TRACE   WRITE

6.

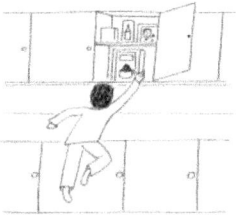

get

7.

fed

8.

yes

9.

get

10.

yes

SET 2.1 - Book 2
GUMDROPS FOR MOPPET TOPS

bartlebysbox.com

PIG IS IN

NAME

DIRECTIONS: Retell the story, trace and write the words.

TRACE   WRITE

1.

pig

2.

sit

3.
 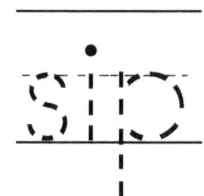
sip

4.
 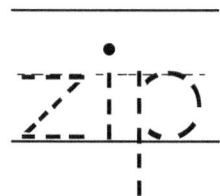
zip

5.
 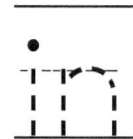
in

SET 2.1 - Book 3
GUMDROPS FOR MOPPET TOPS

bartlebysbox.com

PIG IS IN

NAME

DIRECTIONS: Retell the story, trace and write the words.

TRACE	WRITE

6.

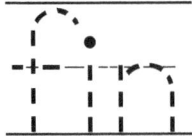

7.

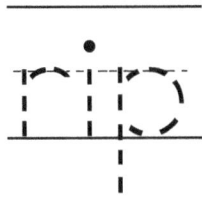

8.

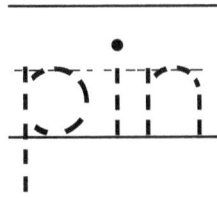

9.

10.

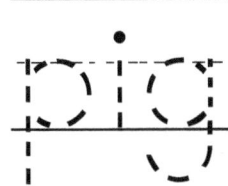

SET 2.1 - Book 3
GUMDROPS FOR MOPPET TOPS

POP

NAME

DIRECTIONS: Retell the story, trace and write the words.

TRACE	WRITE

1.

Tom

2.

Roz

3.

Dot

4.

Mom

5.

pot

SET 2.1 - Book 4
GUMDROPS FOR MOPPET TOPS

bartlebysbox.com

NAME

DIRECTIONS: Retell the story, trace and write the words.

TRACE   WRITE

6.

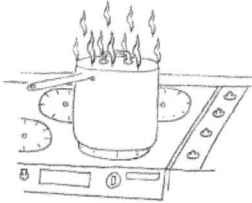   hot

7.

   pop

8.

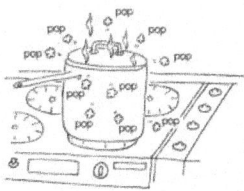   pop

9.

   hot

10.

   mmm

bartlebysbox.com

SUN FUN

NAME

DIRECTIONS: Retell the story, trace and write the words.

TRACE   WRITE

1.

sun

2.

up

3.

run

4.

up

5.

fun

SET 2.1 - Book 5
GUMDROPS FOR MOPPET TOPS

bartlebysbox.com

 SUN FUN

NAME

DIRECTIONS: Retell the story, trace and write the words.

TRACE   WRITE

6.

 up

7.

 run

8.

 up

9.

 fun

10.

 sun

SET 2.1 - Book 5
GUMDROPS FOR MOPPET TOPS
Copyright © 2017 by Mark Linley. All Rights Reserved. MADE IN THE USA

bartlebysbox.com

RAT CAN

NAME

TRACE   WRITE

1.

mat

2.

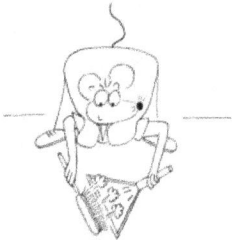
pan

3.

rag

4.

nap

5.

tap

bartlebysbox.com

RAT CAN

NAME _____

DIRECTIONS: Retell the story, trace and write the words.

TRACE WRITE

6.

rag

7.

rat

8.

rag

9.

rag

10.

sat

SET 2.2 - Book 1
GUMDROPS FOR MOPPET TOPS
Copyright © 2017 by Mark Linley. All Rights Reserved. MADE IN THE USA

bartlebysbox.com

 JET

NAME

DIRECTIONS: Retell the story, trace and write the words.

TRACE   WRITE

1.
   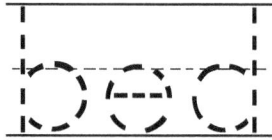 bed

2.
   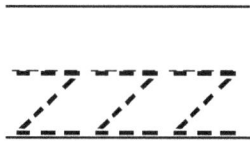 zzz

3.
   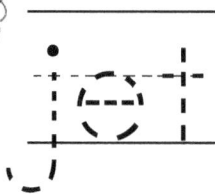 jet

4.
   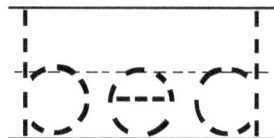 bed

5.
   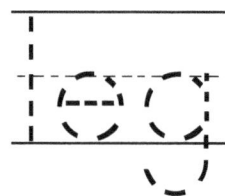 beg

SET 2.2 - Book 2
GUMDROPS FOR MOPPET TOPS
123

bartlebysbox.com

JET

NAME

DIRECTIONS: Retell the story, trace and write the words.

TRACE	WRITE

6.  bed

7.  men

8.  net

9.  yes

10.  bed

SET 2.2 - Book 2
GUMDROPS FOR MOPPET TOPS
Copyright © 2017 by Mark Linley. All Rights Reserved. MADE IN THE USA

 KIDS

NAME

DIRECTIONS: Retell the story, trace and write the words.

TRACE   WRITE

1.

 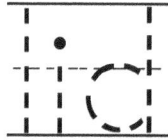 id

2.

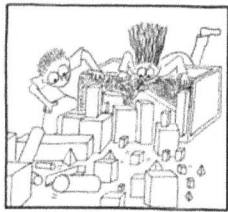 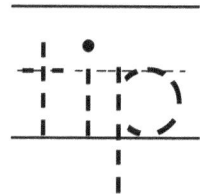 tip

3.

 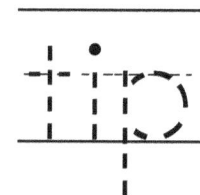 tip

4.

  sit

5.

 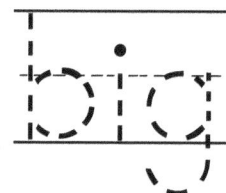 big

SET 2.2 - Book 3
GUMDROPS FOR MOPPET TOPS
Copyright © 2017 by Mark Linley. All Rights Reserved. MADE IN THE USA
125

bartlebysbox.com

KIDS

NAME

DIRECTIONS: Retell the story, trace and write the words.

TRACE   WRITE

6.

 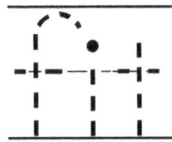

7.

 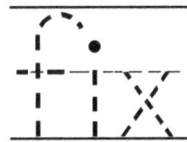

8.

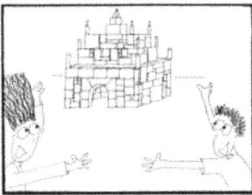 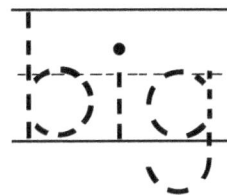

9.

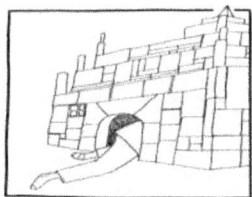 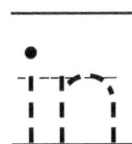

10.

SET 2.2 - Book 3
GUMDROPS FOR MOPPET TOPS
Copyright © 2017 by Mark Linley. All Rights Reserved. MADE IN THE USA

bartlebysbox.com

DOC

NAME

DIRECTIONS: Retell the story, trace and write the words.

TRACE	WRITE

1.
Mom

2.
Tom

3.
hot

4.
Doc

5.
hot

GUMDROPS FOR MOPPET TOPS

bartlebysbox.com

NAME

DIRECTIONS: Retell the story, trace and write the words.

TRACE   WRITE

6.    jot

7.    box

8.    pop

9.    Mom

10.    Tom

RUN

NAME

TRACE   WRITE

1.

run

2.

bus

3.

run

4.

sub

5.

run

SET 2.2 - Book 5
GUMDROPS FOR MOPPET TOPS
Copyright © 2017 by Mark Linley. All Rights Reserved. MADE IN THE USA

bartlebysbox.com

RUN

NAME

DIRECTIONS: Retell the story, trace and write the words.

TRACE   **WRITE**

6.

run

7.

rug

8.

fun

9.

up

10.

hug

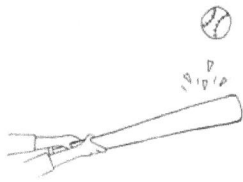

BAM !

NAME

DIRECTIONS: Retell the story, trace and write the words.

TRACE		WRITE

1.

cap

2.

bat

3.

fan

4.

bam

5.

ran

SET 2.3 - Book 1
GUMDROPS FOR MOPPET TOPS

bartlebysbox.com

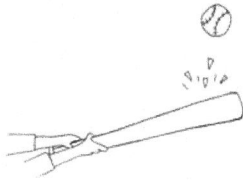

BAM !

NAME

DIRECTIONS: Retell the story, trace and write the words.

TRACE   WRITE

6.

fan

7.

ran

8.

tag

9.

sad

10.

pal

SET 2.3 - Book 1
GUMDROPS FOR MOPPET TOPS
Copyright © 2017 by Mark Linley. All Rights Reserved. MADE IN THE USA

bartlebysbox.com

132

VET

NAME

DIRECTIONS: Retell the story, trace and write the words.

TRACE   WRITE

1.

   Rex

2.

   beg

3.

   get

4.

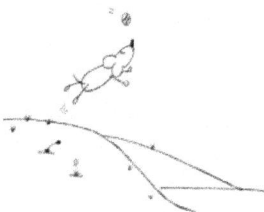   Rex

5.

   yes

133

bartlebysbox.com

VET

NAME

DIRECTIONS: Retell the story, trace and write the words.

TRACE   WRITE

6.

men

7.

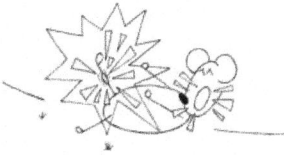
leg

8.

get

9.

vet

10.

bed

SET 2.3 - Book 2
GUMDROPS FOR MOPPET TOPS
Copyright © 2017 by Mark Linley. All Rights Reserved. MADE IN THE USA

bartlebysbox.com

PIG SIPS

NAME

DIRECTIONS: Retell the story, trace and write the words.

TRACE		WRITE

1.  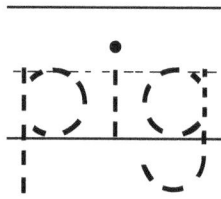 pig

2.  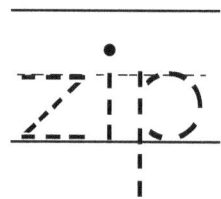 zip

3.   in

4.  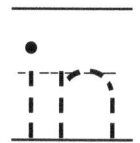 in

5.  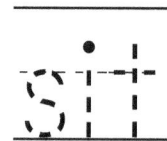 sit

SET 2.3 - Book 3
GUMDROPS FOR MOPPET TOPS

bartlebysbox.com

PIG SIPS

NAME

DIRECTIONS: Retell the story, trace and write the words.

TRACE   WRITE

6.

mix

7.

pig

8.

sip

9.

sip

10.

tip

NAME

_____

- -

_____

DIRECTIONS: Retell the story, trace and write the words.

TRACE WRITE

1.

dog

2.

job

3.

on

4.

hop

5.

dog

SET 2.3 - Book 4
GUMDROPS FOR MOPPET TOPS

 TOP DOG

NAME

DIRECTIONS: Retell the story, trace and write the words.

TRACE   WRITE

6.

hop

7.

hop

8.

dog

9.

hot

10.

dog

FUN FUN FUN

NAME

DIRECTIONS: Retell the story, trace and write the words.

TRACE	WRITE

1.
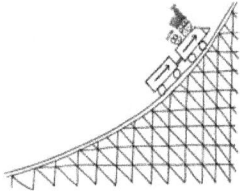
up

2.

hug

3.

yum

4.

fun

5.

sub

SET 2.3 - Book 5
GUMDROPS FOR MOPPET TOPS

bartlebysbox.com

FUN FUN FUN

NAME

DIRECTIONS: Retell the story, trace and write the words.

TRACE		WRITE

6.

tub

7.

bus

8.

fun

9.

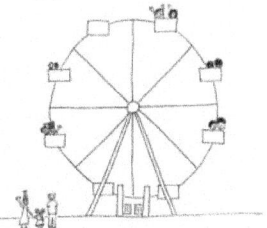

up

10.

us

SET 2.3 - Book 5
GUMDROPS FOR MOPPET TOPS

bartlebysbox.com